D0468288

EUDORA WELTY

Women Writers

General Editors: *Eva Figes and Adele King*

Published titles:

Sylvia Plath, Susan Bassnett
Fanny Burney, Judy Simons
Christina Stead, Diana Brydon
Charlotte Bronte, Pauline Nestor
Margaret Atwood, Barbara Hill Rigney
Eudora Welty, Louise Westling
Anne Bronte, Elizabeth Langland

Forthcoming:

Jane Austen, Meenakshi Mukherjee
Elizabeth Barrett Browning, Majorie Stone
Elizabeth Bowen, Phyllis Lassner
Emily Bronte, Lyn Pykett
Ivy Compton Burnett, Kathy Gentile
Willa Cather, Susie Thomas
Colette, Diana Holmes
Emily Dickinson, Joan Kirkby
George Eliot, Kristin Brady
Mrs Gaskell, Jane Spencer
Doris Lessing, Barbara Hill Rigney
Katherine Mansfield, Diane DeBell
Christina Rossetti, Linda Marshall
Jean Rhys, Carol Rumens
Stevie Smith, Catherine Civello
Muriel Spark, Judith Sproxton
Edith Wharton, Katherine Joslin
Women in Romanticism, Meena Alexander
Virginia Woolf, Clare Hanson

Women Writers

EUDORA WELTY

Louise Westling

BARNES & NOBLE BOOKS
Totowa, New Jersey

© Louise Westling 1989

First published in the United States of America 1989 by
BARNES & NOBLE BOOKS
81 Adams Drive, Totawa, N.J. 07512

ISBN 0–389–20867–1
ISBN 0–389–20868–x (Pbk)

Printed in the People's Republic of China

Library of Congress Cataloging-in-Publication Data
Westling, Louise Hutchings.
    Eudora Welty.
    (Women writers)
    1. Welty, Eudora, 1909– —Criticism and interpretation.
2. Feminism and literature–United States–History–20th
century.   I. Title.   II. Series.
PS3545.E6296 1989   813'.52   88–35139
ISBN 0–389–20867–1
ISBN 0–389–20868–X (pbk.)

Contents

Acknowledgements

I am indebted to the following for their support of this study: Paul Armstrong, Head of the Department of English at the University of Oregon; the Center for the Study of Women in Society at the University; and H. T. Holmes and the staff of the Department of Archives and History of the State of Mississippi in Jackson.

Friends and colleagues gave advice and careful readings of the manuscript as it evolved. My husband George Wickes is first among them, always my most demanding and illuminating editor. Suzanne Marrs welcomed me when I first went to Jackson in June of 1987 to work with Miss Welty's papers, and she has given judicious counsel since, particularly for the first, biographical, chapter of the study. Mary Wood and Paul Armstrong also read parts of the manuscript and provided guidance on matters of critical theory.

Finally I want to thank Eudora Welty for the kindness with which she welcomed me and talked with me about her work during my trips to Jackson in the summer of 1987.

Editors' Preface

The study of women's writing has been long neglected by a male critical establishment both in academic circles and beyond. As a result, many women writers have either been unfairly neglected or have been marginalised in some way, so that their true influence and importance has been ignored. Other women writers have been accepted by male critics and academics, but on terms which seem, to many women readers of this generation, to be false or simplistic. In the past the internal conflicts involved in being a woman in a male-dominated society have been largely ignored by readers of both sexes, and this has affected our reading of women's work. The time has come for a serious reassessment of women's writing in the light of what we understand today.

This series is designed to help in that reassessment.

All the books are written by women because we believe that men's understanding of feminist critique is only, at best, partial. And besides, men have held the floor quite long enough.

EVA FIGES
ADELE KING

1 A Sheltered Life

Eudora Welty has never been comfortable with feminism. She has lived most of her life where she was born, in the settled community of Jackson, Mississippi. Hers has been a social world in which clear distinctions have always existed between the roles of men and women and where the Southern tradition of masculine chivalry has offered courtesy and deference to white women of her class. When interviewers have tried to press her on Women's Liberation or the particular trials of the woman writer, she has resisted. 'I'm not interested in any kind of feminine repartee,' she told Charles Bunting in 1972. 'All that talk of women's lib doesn't apply *at all* to women writers. We've always been able to do whatever we've wished.'[1] Six years later in a conversation with a young woman who championed Tille Olsen's outspoken feminism, Welty agreed that women writers have been at a disadvantage compared to men, but she denied that her own career had been affected by her sex. Always an intensely private person, she said she hated 'the grotesque quality' of the women's movement, feeling that the extreme behaviour of some activists made 'comedians of all of us' and that change could be achieved in quieter ways (*CNVRS*, pp. 250–51).

Welty seems to feel that labels such as 'woman writer' and 'feminist' are narrow and politically charged. She prefers to consider literary achievement as a human creative endeavour unmarked by sex. As she explains in the essay 'Must the Novelist Crusade?', written at the height of the Civil Rights unrest in the 1960s, she feels that preaching of any kind is antithetical to the real work of a novelist, which is to capture human life as it is, not as one might wish it to be according to some general political programme.[2] In answer to a question about her political responsibilities, she told an interviewer bluntly, 'The real crusader doesn't need to crusade; he writes about human beings in the sense Chekhov did. He tries to see a human being whole with all his wrong-headedness and all his right-headedness' (*CNVRS*, p. 226).

Her fiction names and embodies the reality she sees, and her vision is wide. It includes the lives of many kinds of human beings – black and white, male and female, aristo-cratic, middle-class, and rural poor. Her work also ranges in tone and genre, from grotesque satire as in 'Petrified Man' and 'Why I Live at the P.O.' to fairy tale as in *The Robber Bridegroom* and comedy of manners as in *Delta Wedding* and the starker *Optimist's Daughter*. Nevertheless, Eudora Welty's writing is centred in the experience of women, and it is important to consider the ways in which her stories and novels explore the traditional sources of power in women's lives. Much of Welty's best writing dramatises the centrality of the feminine which has been denigrated or marginalised in masculine literary tradition.

She is as uncomfortable with the idea of biography as she is with the feminist movement. She feels that a writer's private life should be kept private, that the work should stand alone (*CNVRS*, p. 81). In a sense she has forestalled any attempts at biography – at least for a time – by writing *One Writer's Beginnings* (1984), a series of three autobiographical essays. In surveying her life, she admits its quiet, protected quality but insists, 'A sheltered life can be a daring life as well. For all serious daring starts from within.'[3] In this regard she is like her much admired predecessor Jane Austen in having spent most of her life modestly in one place, surrounded by family and friends. Her best work is no more limited by those circumstances than Austen's, for both women view their world with a keen satiric gaze which allows them to transform it into a microcosm of the human comedy.

The daughter of a spirited mother and a gentle, protective father, Welty grew up in a household devoted to books and sheltered from squalor and violence. Both of her parents had been country schoolteachers before they married, and they raised their children to revere learning. Her father 'loved all instruments that would instruct and fascinate' and kept a telescope, maps, a magnifying glass, a kaleidoscope, and a gyroscope in a special drawer to use while entertaining his children with astronomy and physics lessons (*OWB*, p. 3). Her mother was a passionate reader who 'sank as a hedonist into novels', 'read Dickens in the spirit in which she would have eloped with him', and read frequently to her avid young daughter in her bedroom rocking chair, before the fire downstairs in winter, at bedtime in the child's own room, and even in the kitchen while churning butter (*OWB*, pp. 5, 7).

Eudora Welty's father, Christian Webb Welty, was of Swiss-German ancestry and had spent a rather lonely boyhood on a farm in southern Ohio. Her mother, Mary Chestina Andrews, came of the English, Scottish, Irish, and French Huguenot background common in the Southern states. Chestina Andrews' father had been a talented and adventurous Virginian who ran away to the mountains of West Virginia at 18, became a lawyer and married the daughter of 'a strongly dedicated Baptist preacher.' Chestina Andrews grew up in the weathered wooden house her father had built on the top of the highest mountain he could find (*OWB*, pp. 46–50). She was the eldest of six children and the only daughter, with a determined and passionate spirit. When she began teaching at the age of 17 in a one-room mountain school, she announced to the children and the parents who had come to inspect her, 'I intend to keep order, and I will cut a switch and take it to anyone who misbehaves.' The rough mountain children

were of all ages, some older and larger than she. When
the parents said, 'What do you intend to do about us?'
Chestina answered, 'I'll whip you too.' The parents liked
her spirit and were satisfied that their children would be
kept under control.[4]

Chestina Andrews met Christian Welty in the summer
of 1903 when he came to her part of West Virginia to work
in the offices of a lumber company. When they married in
1904, they decided to begin their life together in a new
part of the world and chose Jackson, Mississippi, where
Christian began working as a bookkeeper in a new insurance
company. He remained with the Lamar Life Insurance
Company all his life, rising steadily in its ranks until he
became its president not long before his untimely death
of leukemia at the age of 52 (*OWB*, pp. 52, 75; *CNVRS*,
pp. 253, 320).

Eudora Alice Welty was born into a rather anxious
household on 13 April 1909. There had been a baby boy
before the daughter, Chestina Welty had almost died of
septicemia after his birth and the infant had not survived.
Her parents overprotected their daughter in fear of any
repetition of such a disaster. They also sought to shield
her and her two brothers, Edward, born when she was 3,
and Walter, born when she was 6, from the kind of loss that
had marred their own early years. Christian Welty had lost
his mother when he was 7. He had carefully preserved a
little keepsake book where she had written on the day of
her death, 'My dearest Webbie: I want you to be a good
boy and to meet me in heaven. Your loving Mother.' His
daughter says that throughout his life, he 'could never bear
pain very well.' He devoted himself optimistically to the
future, but

along with the energetic practice of optimist, and
deeper than this, was an abiding awareness of mortality
itself – most of all the mortality of a parent. This care,

this caution, that ruled his life in the family, and in the business he chose and succeeded in expanding so far, began very possibly when he was seven years old, when his mother, asking him with perhaps literally her last words to be a good boy and meet her in heaven, died and left him alone (*OWB*, pp. 18, 67, 91).

Chestina Andrews had experienced a similar loss. At the age of 15, she had left her mother and five little brothers at home on their mountain top, to accompany her gravely ill father across an icy river on a raft and then by train to a hospital in Baltimore, where he died of a ruptured appendix. Although she knew not a soul in Baltimore, she had to make arrangements to return home by train with the coffin containing her father's body (*OWB*, p. 51).

Eudora Welty remembers that her mother 'suffered from a morbid streak which in all the life of the family reached out on occasions – the worst occasions – and touched us, clung around us' (*OWB*, p. 17). Her father preferred to concentrate on practical measures to protect his family. He warned them to stay away from windows during electrical storms, he scoured the bottoms of his daughter's new shoes with a pen knife so that she would not slip, and when the family stayed in hotels during their summer trips he carried chains and a coil of rope and an axe into the bedroom every night in case of fire (*OWB*, pp. 4, 18–19, 45).

Because of their care, Welty's parents were able to maintain a safe and contented household for their children. They had a profoundly harmonious marriage which created the domestic atmosphere recollected by their daughter.

When I was young enough to still spend a long time buttoning my shoes in the morning, I'd listen towards the hall: Daddy upstairs was shaving in the bathroom and Mother downstairs was frying the bacon. They would begin whistling back and forth to each other

up and down the stairwell. My father would whistle his
phrase, my mother would try to whistle, then hum hers
back. It was their duet. I drew my buttonhook in and
out and listened to it . . . their song almost floated with
laughter (*OWB*, untitled preface, unpaginated).

The house was full of books and instructive toys. During
exuberant dinner-table arguments, opponents would resolve
their differences by consulting the dictionaries and encyclo-
pedias which lay on a nearby table (*CNVRS*, p. 157; *OWB*,
p. 6). Christian Welty, who was an apostle of progress and
technology, initiated his children into the movements of the
planets and constellations with a telescope in the front yard.
(*OWB*, p. 3). There were clear differences between the
kinds of toys Eudora and her brothers were given, however,
establishing the traditional boundaries between boys and
girls. The boys received erector sets and electric trains,
while Eudora was given dolls which she didn't especially
like.[5] Her major passion was for books, however, and her
parents did not stint in providing them. The treasure she
remembers most vividly was a ten-volume set of children's
books called *Our Wonder World*, given to her when she was
nine. Her favourite volume, *Every Child's Story Book*, contained folktales and myths from all over the world, and she
so saturated herself with these stories that they permanently
shaped her approach to writing her own fiction.[6]

Like most well-brought-up Southern girls, Eudora Welty
learned to play the piano. Her lessons provided experiences
she later drew upon for 'June Recital' in *The Golden Apples*.
She also learned to paint, seriously working with water
colours as a young woman, and in the process training
her eye in ways which became central to the visual quality
of her fiction.[7]

In summer, the family took automobile trips north to
her Welty grandfather's farm in Ohio and her Andrews
grandmother's mountaintop homestead in West Virginia.

The homes of both grandparents left deep impressions on Eudora's mind, but the influence of her grandmother's place was the more formative. Eudora Carden Andrews seems to have been second only to Eudora Welty's mother among the formidable, heroic women who populated her childhood. Her grandmother was a courageous widow who had raised her daughter and five sons and run her farm alone after the death of her husband. The place where she lived seemed a magic one to her granddaughter.

It took the mountain top . . . to give me the sensation of independence. It was as if I'd discovered something I'd never tasted before in my short life. Or rediscovered it – for I associated it with the taste of the water that came out of the well, accompanied with the ring of that long metal sleeve against the sides of the living mountain, as from deep down it was wound up to view brimming and streaming long drops behind it like bright stars on a ribbon. . . . The coldness, the far, unseen, unheard springs of what was in my mouth now, the iron strength of its flavor that drew my cheeks in, its fern-laced smell, all said mountain, mountain, mountain as I swallowed. . . .

It seems likely to me now that the very element in my character that took possession of me there on top of the mountain, the fierce independence that was suddenly mine, to remain inside me no matter how it scared me when I tumbled, was an inheritance. Indeed it was my chief inheritance from my mother, who was braver. . . .It was what we shared, it made the strongest bond between us and the strongest tension (*OWB*, pp. 57, 60).

The powerful bond that her grandmother's place forged between her mother and herself links three generations of women with the kind of wide, sweeping landscape Ellen

Moers identified some years ago as a preeminent symbolic place for feminine assertion.[8] Chestina Welty's behaviour seems to support Moers's point, for she loved storms on the mountain and would scoff at her husband's caution, 'I wasn't a bit afraid of a little lightning and thunder! I'd go out on the mountain and spread my arms wide and *run* in a good big storm!' (*OWB*, p. 4) Landscapes of this kind, with similar associations of female kinship and power, perform a critical symbolic function in Eudora Welty's fiction.

The distinctive traditional position of women in the South is an important backdrop for the strong women in Welty's family and in the Mississippi world of her childhood. The 'Southern belle' was the pride of the region from the middle of the nineteenth century through the early decades of our own. As W. J. Cash put it in *The Mind of the South* (1941),

> She was the South's Palladium, this Southern woman – the shield-bearing Athena gleaming whitely in the clouds, the standard for its rallying, the mystic symbol of its nationality in the face of the foe. She was the lily-pure maid of Astolat and the hunting goddess of the Boetian hill. And – she was the pitiful Mother of God. Merely to mention her name was to send strong men into tears – or shouts.[9]

This ideal placed special burdens on Southern white women – for it only applied to them and indeed only to those of the upper classes – but it also gave them special strengths. The social and political reality which stood behind it was tangled and morally questionable. The position of the Southern lady is in many ways an especially long-lived version of the Victorian situation of women in England and Europe, with all its attendant ironies. Unique complications existed in the Southern situation, however, because of the South's peculiar racial institution. As the region grew defensive in response to national pressures, the white female representative of Christian virtues was lauded in public to divert attention from problems of slavery and racism. She was forced to represent a racial purity which was required by her men for the maintenance of their caste but which many of them regularly transgressed in their own sexual adventures with black women.

In the context of the problems of slavery and miscegenation for which the Southern patriarchy was responsible, the Southern lady held a position of moral superiority. She was painfully aware of the hypocrisy of her father, brothers and husband; they knew it and guiltily acceded influence to her. Thus behind the facade of the Southern patriarchy lay a domestic situation close to matriarchy, as white men sought to exercise the chivalry in their domestic lives which they claimed so proudly in public. Perhaps another consequence of this situation was a tolerance for eccentricity in upper-class white women and a respected place for single women of definite character. Eudora Welty's father was a northerner whose behaviour matched his professed morals, and so the moral blackmail endemic to many polite white households was not a factor in her family. Her mother and grandmother were, however, as we have seen, Southern women of strong character. Young Eudora encountered many of the eccentric but highly respected spinsters of Southern society in her childhood.

The Welty family lived in the heart of the small Mississippi city of Jackson, directly across the street from Davis School and only a few blocks from the new state capitol building, the high school, and the library. During Eudora's childhood years, awesome women presided over the major social institutions she encountered: Jefferson Davis Elementary School, Central High School, and the public library. Preeminent among them was Miss Lorena Duling, Principal of Davis School, whom Welty describes as 'a lifelong subscriber to perfection' who seemed so all-powerful that 'she was like something almost supernatural.' In the mornings when it was time for school to begin, Miss Duling stood in front of Davis school ringing a large brass bell which seemed to grow 'directly out of her right arm, as wings grew out of an angel or a tail out of the devil.' The children believed that she 'could freeze you, maybe kill you, with the look of her eyes' and that she kept a whipping machine in her office.

Miss Duling had come to Mississippi from Kentucky as a sort of educational missionary, because then as now Mississippi was the poorest state in the nation, and early in the century it suffered from a severely underdeveloped educational system. She had so firmly established her authority with three generations of Jackson citizens who had been her students that whenever she wanted a civic problem solved, 'she telephoned the mayor, or the chief of police, or the president of the power company, or the head doctor at the hospital, or the judge in charge of a case, or whoever, and calling them by their first names, *told* them' what to do. She usually won her point (*OWB*, pp. 22–4; *CNVRS*, pp. 205, 291, 294).

Other memorable teachers at Davis School included the music teacher Miss Johnson, who reacted to one of the rare snowstorms to occur in Mississippi by throwing open the window and holding out her black cape to capture snowflakes, then running up and down the aisles of children's desks to display them before the snow melted. Miss Eyrich, the physical training teacher, terrified little Eudora with the military rigour of her direction of games and races. In contrast, the gentle art teacher Miss Ascher purred encouragement as she glided up and down the aisles inspecting the children's efforts. All these women were unmarried, because the profession of schoolteaching was closed to married women in most parts of the United States until after the Second World War.

The one teacher Welty remembers who had been married was the frightening widow Mrs McWille, a heavy, stern lady dressed in black, 'with a high net collar and velvet ribbon, . . . with black circles under her eyes and a mournful, Presbyterian expression.' This monument overheard Eudora and a friend making Saturday plans from adjoining cubicles in the girls' bathroom. 'Can you come spend the day with me?' asked Eudora. The friend replied, 'I might could.' That sub-standard verb brought an immediate response in heavily measured tones: 'Who — said — MIGHT — COULD?' Welty recalls that 'It sounded like "Fe Fi Fo Fum"!' (*OWB*, pp. 27–8).

The librarian of Jackson's Carnegie Library was another commanding female guardian of propriety. 'I never knew anyone who'd grown up in Jackson without being afraid of Mrs Calloway,' Welty remembers. Like a dragon she sat at her desk, facing the front door, and refused entrance to any girl whose skirt could be seen through. She allowed patrons to take out only two books at a time and refused to accept them back until at least a day later (*OWB*, pp. 29–30).

Disciplined in childhood by such demanding authorities, Eudora Welty and her friends from Davis School had no trouble adapting to more advanced studies when they went on to Central High School. They seem to have received unusually sound preparation at Central, because many of Welty's high school friends went on to distinguished careers as composers, journalists, and literary figures in New York (*CNVRS*, pp. 201–206). She herself longed to travel away from Jackson for college, but her parents felt that at 16 she was too young to live far from home. In 1925 she entered Mississippi State College for Women, about 150 miles away in Columbus. It was one of many such institutions in the American South created late in the nineteenth century to give young women the opportunity for university education which had been formerly available only to men. Although Welty was popular at MSCW and

active in student publications, she still felt the need for
wider experience. Her father, considering Midwestern
universities the most progressive, encouraged her to go
to the University of Wisconsin. She transferred there
in 1927 for her final two years, specialising in English
literature. Her classes introduced her to traditional poets
like Swift and Donne, and as she explored the stacks of
the huge university library, she discovered newer writers
such as Yeats, Woolf, Joyce and Faulkner on her own.
At the same time she was discovering her own vocation
for literature.[10]

By the time she knew she wanted to become a writer, she
says, 'It was my mother who emotionally and imaginatively
supported me in my wish.' Her father was sympathetic but
thought she could not support herself by writing and had
better prepare herself to earn a living by more practical
means. 'I had longed to go to New York for a year, so that
was the answer: I went to Columbia [University] School of
Business and had a year in New York' (*CNVRS*, p. 177).

The city of New York offered much more than the
classrooms did. She found that her courses in advertising
required no study, and so she was able to steep herself in
the cultural ferment of that period in New York.

Everybody that was wonderful was then at their peak.
People like Noel Coward, all the wonderful music hall
stars – Beatrice Lillie, Bert Lahr, Fred Allen, both the
Astaires, Jack Benny, Joe Cook, and Ed Wynn. Wonderful dramatic stars, even Nazimova! Katherine Cornell,
the Lunts – if I sat down to it, I could make a list of everybody on God's earth that was playing. Martha Graham
was dancing solo in a little cubbyhole somewhere. I would
go and watch her dance. And Shan-Kar! Everybody
was there. For somebody who had never, in a sustained
manner, been to the theater or to the Metropolitan
Museum, where I went every Sunday, it was just a

cornucopia. We had a good group of people from Jackson there at Columbia to start with, so we had company for everything we wanted to do. We could set forth any-where. We could go dancing in Harlem to Cab Calloway. We went a lot to Small's Paradise, a night-club in Harlem where all the great bands were playing then; whites were welcome as anybody else (*CNVRS*, pp. 217–18).

In 1931, as the Great Depression settled in upon the country, Welty's life in New York came to an abrupt end. Her father fell suddenly ill with leukemia, and she returned to Jackson to be with her family. Christian Welty died in a matter of weeks at the age of 52 (*CNVRS*, p. 178). Eudora and her mother were in the hospital with him at the end, when there was a desperate attempt to give him a blood transfusion. Welty describes her mother's effort to save her husband as he had saved her life after the birth of their first child. Both parents lay on cots, side by side, and a tube was run from Chestina Welty's arm to her husband's.

My father, I believe, was unconscious. My mother was looking at him. I could see her fervent face: there was no doubt as to what she was thinking. This time *she* would save *his* life, as he'd saved hers so long ago, when she was dying of septicemia. . . . All at once his face turned dusky red all over. The doctor made a disparaging sound with his lips, the kind a woman knitting makes when she drops a stitch. What the doctor meant by it was that my father had died.

Chestina Welty never recovered emotionally from the loss (*OWB*, pp. 92–3).

Christian Welty's death meant that his daughter had to earn a living. Her two brothers were still in school, and the Depression had eroded the liberal insurance provisions he had made for his family (*OWB*, p. 91). Eudora definitely did not want to go into the one profession which seemed her obvious destiny. She feared that teaching would trap her and felt she lacked 'the instructing turn of mind, the selflessness, the patience' necessary (*OWB*, p. 82). Instead she took whatever small jobs she could find in writing and advertising. For a time she wrote the schedule and the newsletter and various scripts for Mississippi's first radio station, WJDX, which her father had established in the clock tower of his life insurance building. She did freelance writing for local newspapers and was one of a group of friends who tried to start a new paper in an attic over a store where the heat was so intense that 'it was like working inside a popcorn popper' (*CNVRS*, pp. 202–204).

Welty's first full-time and fully-paid job was that of a publicity agent for the Works Progress Administration, established by the Roosevelt administration in 1933 to create jobs and unify the demoralised nation. WPA workers built bridges and roads and public buildings; WPA writers and photographers fanned out along the nation's roads to survey its farmlands and describe its towns and cities; WPA artists and musicians created works in every imaginable medium. Alfred Kazin describes the work of WPA agents as 'a repository as well as a symbol of the reawakened American sense of its own history', which uncovered 'an America that nothing in the academic histories had ever prepared one for, and very little in imaginative writing.'[11]

In many of the same ways in which the WPA initiated a process of national self-discovery, Eudora Welty's job began a personal awakening for her. She has often said that it opened her eyes as a writer to the resources of her native state. She travelled, usually by public bus but sometimes by car, all through the state's towns and rural areas, interviewing local officials about public projects, setting up booths in county fairs, writing newspaper reports about civic events. The poverty and hardship of rural life, as well as the strength of the country people, struck her deeply. Much of what she encountered became material for her early short stories (*CNVRS*, p. 154–7).

As she travelled, Welty took over 1200 photographs of ordinary people at their daily routines of work and recreation. She did this on her own, not as part of her WPA duties, and she developed the pictures herself in her own kitchen. This was a serious avocation which resulted in some of the best documentary photographs of black southerners taken during the Depression era. Welty tried unsuccessfully for a number of years in the late 1930s and 1940s to have a collection of the photographs published, and succeeded only in having a one woman show in 1936 at a small gallery on Madison Avenue in New York. A selection of 100 of the pictures was published in 1971 as *One Time, One Place*.

Photography trained Welty's vision, by focusing and fixing information in precise images, teaching her to see human emotion as it is expressed in movement, and helping her understand how to capture the transient moment. 'Making pictures of people in all sorts of situations,' she wrote in *One Writer's Beginnings*, 'I learned that every feeling waits upon its gesture; and I had to be prepared to recognize this moment when I saw it. These were things a story writer needed to know' (pp. 84–5).

During this same period in the mid-1930s, she was training herself as a writer, using rural Mississippi people and landscapes as her subjects. At the suggestion of Hubert Creekmore, a friend and neighbour who was himself a writer, she sent two stories to a small literary magazine called *Manuscript*.[12] In March of 1936, she received a surprising response from its editor. 'Without any hesitation,' wrote John Rood, 'we can say that DEATH OF A TRAVELING SALESMAN is one of the best stories that has come to our attention – and one of the best stories we have ever read. It is superbly done. And MAGIC is only slightly short of it in quality.' Rood and his co-editor and wife Mary Lawhead accepted both stories and published 'Death of a Traveling Salesman' almost at once.

Three days after the story appeared, Harold Strauss at the New York publishing firm of Covici-Friede wrote her a letter praising the story and urging her to send him some of her work and a description of her literary plans. When she proposed a collection of short stories, however, he responded with the discouraging news that 'it is quite impossible to publish a volume of stories by a relatively unknown author under the present conditions of the book market.' Instead, Strauss urged, she should try to write a novel. This was to be the standard response from publishers for four years, as Welty continued publishing short stories in increasingly prestigious literary journals including *The Southern Review* and *The Prairie Schooner*. Robert Penn Warren and Cleanth Brooks of *The Southern Review* were especially encouraging. But New York publishing houses continued to press for a novel, despite Welty's increasing reputation and the national prizes her stories began to win. She travelled to New York a number of times over a three- or four-year period, to try to sell a collection of stories illustrated by her photographs, but without success.[13]

Harold Strauss wrote her the most telling criticism late in 1937, describing qualities which are still criticised in Welty's fiction but which may well have more to do with her feminine perspective or her modernist exploration of subtle, interior experience than with literary value.

Regarding the stories themselves, they show an acute but somewhat unfocussed sensibility. They are charming but vague. Sometimes the architecture of the stories is at war with the content. The architecture is dynamic, but the purport of most of your stories is simply the creation of a mood. Often you have no story to tell at all, but rather a state of mind to convey.[14]

Strauss went on to say that he thought these problems could be solved by Welty's writing a novel.

Under such pressures, Welty began writing a novel called *The Cheated*. In September of 1938, she submitted it to Houghton-Mifflin. It was speedily rejected, on the grounds that its 'architecture' was bad and that 'you have apprehended rather than thought out the situations and characters, with the result that much of the story has the quality of a dream or fantasy.'[15] Such an effect may have been exactly what Welty intended, for it characterises her first long piece of fiction, *The Robber Bridegroom*, which was published four years later and received some reviewers' strongest praise at the time.

The novel's rejection was balanced by *The Southern Review*'s continued interest in her short stories and the encouragement of Katherine Anne Porter, a highly esteemed Southern writer whose praise gave the young woman a tremendous boost.[16] Then in November of 1938, Ford Madox Ford wrote, at Porter's urging, to request that Welty send some of her fiction to him so that he might try to help her place it with a publisher. When he read her work, he responded with praise for her 'very remarkable gift' and promised to try to find a publisher for a collection of stories. Ford began sending her work to publishers in London, but he died in mid-1939, before he was able to pursue the project further.[17]

At the end of that year, however, Welty's angel appeared in the person of a dashing, teasing, and appreciative editor, John Woodburn of Doubleday. On a scouting trip through the South, Woodburn came through Jackson and visited with Eudora and her mother. He returned to New York with a bundle of her stories which he liked and tried unsuccessfully to sell. Woodburn also found her an agent, Diarmuid Russell, the son of the Irish poet A. E. (George Russell). During the following year, Russell placed some of her stories with the large national magazines *Harper's*,

Harper's Bazaar, and *The Atlantic Monthly*, and he became an invaluable adviser throughout her career, as well as a lifelong friend.

Welty sent the manuscript of her first novel, *The Robber Bridegroom*, to Woodburn, who responded in November of 1940, saying he found it 'a very savory dish' but thought it should be the *hors d'oeuvres* preceding an *entrée*. What he had in mind was a collection of Mississippi stories. By January of 1941, he had succeeded in persuading Doubleday to publish Welty's first collection of stories, *A Curtain of Green. The Robber Bridegroom* was saved for publication until the following year.[18] Welty's publishing career was at last underway; she would never again have to struggle for acceptance.

Recognition brought prizes and opportunities for travel and for employment in New York. Welty continued to live in Jackson with her mother but made regular forays to the North. In 1940 she won a fellowship to the prestigious Bread Loaf Writers' Conference in Middlebury, Vermont. The next year she spent the summer in residence at Yaddo, the artists' colony in New York state which drew such writers as Langston Hughes, Katherine Anne Porter, Carson McCullers, Robert Lowell and Flannery O'Connor. Welty won a second prize in the O. Henry Awards for her story 'A Worn Path' in 1941, and a first prize in the O. Henry Awards as well as a Guggenheim Fellowship in 1942. She won another O. Henry first prize in 1943 and was the first person ever to win two in succession. The American Academy of Arts and Letters granted her a $1000 award in 1944, and she spent the summer of that year living in New York City as a staff writer for the *New York Times Book Review*.[19]

Meanwhile she continued producing new fiction. A second collection of short stories appeared in 1943 called *The Wide Net and Other Stories*. During the Allied invasion of Italy in 1944, Welty began writing a novel and sending it

section by section to her friend John Robinson to cheer him
up as he flew missions over the battlefronts and watched in
horror as friends were killed all around him.[20] The novel
was set in Robinson's part of Mississippi – the wide, flat
alluvial plain called the Delta – and was designed to explore
the life of a cotton-farming family during a period when no
public events invaded the peaceful cycle of domestic and
agricultural life. It was an antidote to war, a celebration
of community and renewal symbolised by marriage. In
1946 the novel was published as *Delta Wedding* to a mixed
response from critics, some finding it dull and plotless and
others praising it as similar in style to the work of Virginia
Woolf and Elizabeth Bowen. Bowen herself reviewed *Delta
Wedding* for *The Tatler*, praising it and hoping that the novel
would achieve the status of a classic. The novel reached the
American best seller list in May of 1946.[21]

In August of 1947, Welty participated in the week-
long Northwest Writers' Conference at the University
of Washington in Seattle. The experience was such a
success and she liked the Pacific Coast so much that she
decided to spend the rest of that year in San Francisco.
Her friend John Robinson was studying English literature
in the graduate programme of the University of California
in Berkeley, across San Francisco Bay, so she could see
him from time to time, in addition to enjoying the city. She
walked up and down its steep streets, exploring Chinatown
and the beaches, savouring the atmosphere which became
the setting for 'Music from Spain', the only story in *The
Golden Apples* to take place outside of Mississippi.[22]

In 1949, Welty published *The Golden Apples*, a collection
of short stories set in a small Mississippi town called
Morgana and so closely related that they constitute a loose
novel like Hemingway's *In Our Time* and Faulkner's *Go
Down, Moses*. That year she also won another Guggenheim
Fellowship, that enabled her to travel on the Continent and
in Britain. In Paris she heard that Elizabeth Bowen admired

her work and had expressed a wish to meet her. When Welty reached Dublin, she gathered up her courage and wrote a note to Bowen, asking if she might call on her. Bowen responded with an invitation to come down to County Cork and spend the weekend at Bowen's Court. That was the beginning of a friendship that lasted until Bowen's death and brought the two together numerous times at Bowen's Court and in Jackson, when Bowen visited the United States.[23]

Through the 1950s Welty continued producing new fiction steadily and accumulating more honours. She won another O. Henry prize in 1951 and was elected to the National Institute of Arts and Letters in 1952. In 1954 she published *Selected Stories* and *The Ponder Heart*, a comic short novel, in which a spinster niece recounts the amorous career of her pathologically generous Uncle Daniel Ponder, who accidentally tickles his young wife to death in a thunderstorm while attempting to take her mind off her fright. In 1955 she received the William Dean Howells Medal of the Academy of Arts and Letters for *The Ponder Heart* and published another collection of new stories, *The Bride of Innisfallen*.[24] She had travelled in Europe and Britain a second time in 1952, and she returned in 1954 to participate in a six-week conference on American studies at Cambridge University. There she delivered a lecture on 'Place in Fiction' which has since become a classic statement of the central function of physical settings in fiction. The Cambridge programme was repeated for five years, and Welty was the first woman to be invited. She was also the first woman to enter the hall of Peterhouse College, when she was invited to a special dinner.

Women weren't allowed there. They were so dear the way they told me: they said, 'Miss Welty, you are invited to come to this, but we must tell you that we debated for a long time about whether or not we should ask you. No woman has ever crossed the threshold, including Queen

Victoria, who *demanded* to and was refused.' And I thought, well now, what would be the correct thing for me to do, they having given me this leave? And then I thought, I'm going to do it. They've already decided that I can, and I think to back out would sort of demean the *greatness*, the *momentousness*, of this invitation. Besides, I was curious.[25]

During 1948 and 1949, Welty and her friend John Robinson had collaborated on a screenplay of *The Robber Bridegroom*. By 1952, *The Robber Bridegroom* was being turned into a musical by Baldwin Bergersen and William Archibald, when Archibald suddenly died. The project was completed much later by Alfred Uhry and Robert Waldman.[26] A new theatrical project developed in the mid-1950s, however, which came to fruition as a modestly successful Broadway play of *The Ponder Heart* in 1956. During this same period, Welty's mother began to suffer from serious eye problems. As the play was being written and staged in 1955, an eye operation was required for Mrs Welty.[27] Although she recovered in time, her vision and her health began a decline which required closer attention from her daughter. By the 1960s, family health problems were keeping Eudora close to home and making it difficult for her to do uninterrupted work on her writing. She did some lecturing and wrote shorter pieces, publishing *Three Papers on Fiction* in 1962 and a children's book, *The Shoe Bird*, in 1964. She was also at work on a novel which eventually took ten years to write and was published in 1970 as *Losing Battles* (*CNVRS*, p. 81). Both Chestina Welty and Eudora's brother Edward died in 1966. In part as a way of coming to terms with those experiences, she wrote a short novel, *The Optimist's Daughter*, whose central presence is a woman who shares much with Chestina Andrews Welty. Indeed the novel is dedicated to her and contains autobiographical material from Eudora's childhood visits to West Virginia as well

as material from Mrs Welty's life. As Eudora Welty makes
clear in several interviews, however, these materials have
been reshaped for fictional purposes (*CNVRS*, pp. 116,
174–5, 212–16, 239–42, 252–3).

Welty's selection of Depression-era photographs, *One
Time, One Place*, was published in 1971, and *The Optimist's
Daughter* was published in 1972, winning a Pulitzer Prize
the following year. In 1978 she published a collection of
her non-fiction pieces, *The Eye of the Story*, followed two
years later by *The Collected Stories of Eudora Welty*. An
old friend at Harvard University persuaded her to deliver
the William E. Massey lectures there in 1983, which she
revised and published in 1984 as *One Writer's Beginnings*.
These memoirs became a surprising commercial success,
the almost unheard-of phenomenon of a university press
book that made the best seller list.

Throughout the 1970s and 1980s, Welty has been
inundated by invitations to lecture and teach at universities
around the United States. Numerous academic conferences
have been held on her work, she has been made a member
of the American Academy of Arts and Letters, and she
has been awarded many honorary degrees by institutions
ranging from the University of Wisconsin to Smith College.
She has been a writer-in-residence at many universities,
including Oxford and Cambridge in England. She received
medals from both President Jimmy Carter and President
Ronald Reagan, and in 1987 she was made a Chevalier de
l'Ordre des Arts et Lettres by the French government. As
Welty's fiction achieved its place in the canon of American
fiction, academic interviewers importuned her in increasing
numbers, and she responded with characteristic generosity.
More than twenty interviews, the best of which come in the
years after the publication of *Losing Battles*, were collected
and published in 1984 by Peggy Whitman Prenshaw as
Conversations with Eudora Welty. They provide a vivid sense
of Eudora Welty as a person and an informal collection of

her views on the writing process, literary values, and her own work.

Eudora Welty continues to live quietly among her neighbours in Jackson, but by now she is such a local celebrity that she is recognised everywhere with discreet proprietary affection. Strangers driving alongside her car in the streets of Jackson will look over and smile, even wave. She has won this place in her native town by a lifetime of careful craft and such a modest response to her fame that she is accorded a protective courtesy.

2 A Generous Comic Muse

Eudora Welty is a writer of remarkable technical versatility whose essential mode is comic and whose favourite subject is the family. Most of her fiction is written from the perspective of female observers or participants in domestic life, and the writers closest to her in craft and kinship of feeling are Anton Chekhov, Jane Austen, Virginia Woolf, Katherine Anne Porter, and Elizabeth Bowen. Welty's comedy of manners ranges from grotesque satire in many early stories, to the gentle pastoralism of *Delta Wedding*, to the zany farce of *The Ponder Heart*. 'Comedy is sociable and positive, and exacting,' she has said, and that definition clearly applies to her own fiction.[1]

In *One Writer's Beginnings*, Welty describes an early experience which helped to determine her narrative orientation. Bedridden for some months at the age of 6 or 7 with a mysterious ailment, she was allowed to stay in her parents' bed until they were ready to sleep. There she would lie, feigning sleep and listening to the murmur of her mother's and father's voices as they sat talking in another part of the room. She felt the security of being a hidden observer.

> I don't remember that any secrets were revealed to me, nor do I remember any vivid curiosity on my part to learn something I wasn't supposed to. . . . But I was present in the room with the chief secret there was – the two of them, father and mother, sitting there as one. . . .

24

What I felt was not that I was excluded from them but that I was included, in – and because of – what I could hear of their voices and what I could see of their faces. . . .

I suppose I was exercising as early as then the turn of mind, the nature of temperament, of a privileged observer; and owing to the way I became so, it turned out that I became the loving kind (pp. 20–21).

This memory defines her sympathetic perspective on the human subjects who people her stories, and accounts for the settings and themes that preoccupy her in much of her work. Again and again she writes of the family in its domestic setting, exploring the intimate and communal relationships among its members. She believes, as she feels Jane Austen did before her, 'that the interesting situations of life can take place, and notably do, at home', and 'that the unit of everything worth knowing in life is in the family, that family relationships are the natural basis of all other relationships'. And so her typical story explores the strength of family bonds and tests them under stress (*Eye*, pp. 5, 7; and *OWB*, pp. 86–7). Central to the family is the union of wife and husband and the emotions that animate it. As a loving observer she has celebrated the joy of erotic union, the bonds between parents and children, the cohesiveness and resilience of the family network. She has also explored the causes and consequences of the failure of these bonds, in the destructive passions of jealousy, rage, and fear. Thus stories of suicide and murder like 'Clytie' and 'Flowers for Marjorie' depict the potential violence of family relationships. Much more characteristic, however, are the sustained explorations of successful family networks in her major novels – *Delta Wedding*, *The Optimist's Daughter*, and *Losing Battles*. While the inevitable domestic tensions exist in the Fairchild clan of the first family novel, among the McKelvas of *The Optimist's Daughter*, and in the huge

Renfro reunion of *Losing Battles*, the ultimate emphasis of each novel is positive and celebratory.

Her apprenticeship led her only indirectly to these subjects and to a distinctive use of fairytale and myth. In *One Writer's Beginnings*, she explains that she began by investigating the magnetic attraction she has always felt towards transient artists – 'towards the transience as much as the artists.' At the same time she discovered a fascination with the structure of the family, the mystery of human relationships, and the way in which distinct 'interior visions' guide different people and 'marvelously meet and converge upon the same single exterior object.' From then on, 'vision, dream, illusion, hallucination, obsession, and that most wonderful interior vision which is memory' have been central to the formation and motivating energy of her stories (*OWB*, pp. 86–9). Through experimentation in her first novel, *The Robber Bridegroom*, and in her second volume of short stories, *The Wide Net*, she learned to translate the exotic, fantastic qualities of Mississippi's pioneer history and its folkways into a fiction that used techniques from fable, fairytale, and myth. The progress of her career marks a circular movement from realism through fairytale and myth, to an integration of the real and the mythic, and finally back to the spare realism of *The Optimist's Daughter*.

One Writer's Beginnings does not comment on the influence of other writers on her own development, and Welty resists the efforts of critics to draw simple lines of influence from one writer to another, stressing the highly personal process involved in composing fiction.

You don't start by saying, 'These ingredients are to go in my novel: A, B, C, 1, 2, 3,' and so on. It has to start from an internal feeling of your own and an experience of your own, and I think each reality like that has to find and build its own form. Another person's form doesn't,

may not, even apply. I know it doesn't help in the act
of writing because you're not thinking of anything then
but your story. You're not thinking, 'How did Joyce do
this?' That's fatal   (*CNVRS*, p. 44).

She does admit, however, that reading the work of other
writers opens new perspectives, suggests new techniques
of writing, and generally invigorates the imaginative life.
But the process of absorbing literary experience, like the
apprehension of ordinary reality, is a subtle one which
reshapes such materials as it embraces them. As she puts
it, 'fiction amalgamates with all kinds of other things. When
it comes out as fiction, it's been through a whole mill of
interior life, ...'[2]

Occasionally in interviews she has mentioned some of
the lessons she learned from other writers: the importance
of mastering the cheerful confusion of family life from Jane
Austen, the subtle use of the concrete and particular from
Chekhov, the relation of houses to human character from
Faulkner and practical lessons in narrative construction
from E.M. Forster's *Aspects of the Novel* (*Eye*, pp. 7,
63; *CNVRS*, p. 220). Nevertheless, Welty adapted these
techniques for her own purposes in shaping her own
forms.

Especially important to her distinctive voice and approach
as a writer are traditions of women's writing of which
she seems not to be consciously aware. Feminist literary
historian Ellen Moers argues in *Literary Women* that a
creative interdependence is critical for women writers.
Moers presents striking evidence of such interrelationships
in the nineteenth century, demonstrating the cheerful
competition Jane Austen felt with the now-forgotten Mary
Brunton over the theme of self-control, describing George
Eliot's *Adam Bede* as a kind of lower-middle-class revision
of Austen's *Emma*, and defending Emily Dickinson's
'borrowings' from Elizabeth Barrett Browning's *Aurora*

Leigh as complementary elaborations of themes in the original. Moers's point is that women writers provide each other with a complex imaginative validation of their experience which is lacking in the masculine literary tradition.[3] While Eudora Welty resists such theories, her answer to a male interviewer's question about why there have been 'so few really great women writers' is revealing.

> Well, I think there have been not a few great women writers, of course. Jane Austen. I don't see how anyone could have a greater scope than Jane Austen. Consider Virginia Woolf. The Brontës. Well, you know as many as I do: great women writers. I'm not interested in any kind of a feminine repartee. I don't *care* what sex people are when they write. I just want the result to be a good book   (*CNVRS*, p. 54).

Welty's response is ambivalent. First, in response to the questioner's condescension, she defends the achievements of women writers; then she backs away, dissociating herself from feminism. Yet all the writers she mentions are distinctively feminine in their treatment of theme, point of view, and setting.

Virginia Woolf's feminism in particular is so central to her entire creative life that it is difficult to imagine Welty's failing to respond to it, especially when we realise the trememdous impact Woolf's writing had on her as a young woman.

> She was the one who opened the door. When I read *To the Lighthouse*, I felt, Heavens, *what is this?* I was so excited by the experience I couldn't sleep or eat. . . .

> That beautiful mind! That was the thing. Lucid, passionate, independent, acute, proudly and incessantly

nourished, eccentric for honorable reasons, sensitive for every reason, it has marked us forever. Hers was a sensitivity beside which a Geiger counter is a child's toy made of a couple of tin cans and a rather common piece of string (*CNVRS*, p. 75; *Eye*, p. 191).

The technical surprises which greeted Welty in *To the Lighthouse* were available elsewhere, for Woolf herself had been profoundly influenced by Proust and Joyce. But the differences between Woolf and Joyce suggest why Welty found her particularly compelling.

Virginia Woolf deliberately rejected the masculine tradition of a central narrative consciousness and the author's full access to characters' minds. In *Jacob's Room*, for example, she views European traditions of heroism from the outside – from the excluded female position – so that Jacob's male mind is almost completely unknown. He is presented as an enigma, and our sense of him is delineated by the shapes around that mystery. Through most of the novel the narrator is unsure, looking in on him from outside the rooms in which he lives and works, not daring to conjecture about his inner life.[4]

As an alternative to the masculine literary tradition, Woolf sought to fulfil in her fiction the goals she projects for women writers in *A Room of One's Own* when she says that 'the resources of the English language would be much put to the stretch, and whole flights of words would need to wing their way illegitimately into existence before a woman could say what happens when she goes into a room.'[5] Woolf learned how to say what happens when Mrs Ramsay and scores of other women characters go into a room. She developed strategies for making women's consciousness and women's experiences central to the mainstream of fiction as they had never been before.

With *Delta Wedding*, we can see how Welty absorbed Woolf's example in *To the Lighthouse* into her understanding of narrative point of view and how it informed her vision of family life centred on the mother. *Delta Wedding*, in many respects Eudora Welty's greatest achievement, testifies to creative interdependence between women writers that stands in marked contrast to the antagonistic, Oedipal conflict between individual male writers and their literary 'fathers' described in Harold Bloom's *The Anxiety of Influence*.[6]

A more practical kind of feminine support came from Katherine Anne Porter, an older Southerner who was already a highly respected writer when Eudora Welty began to publish her stories. Porter read Welty's early fiction, admired it, and adopted the young Mississippian as her protégée. Welty remembers her own shyness at that time.

Of course, Katherine Anne Porter was wonderfully generous to me from the beginning. At the time I began sending my first stories to *The Southern Review*, she read them and wrote to me from Baton Rouge inviting me to come down and see her. It took me, I suppose, six months or a year to fully get up my nerve. Twice I got as far as Natchez and turned around and came back. But I finally did get there, and Katherine Anne couldn't have been more welcoming. Later on, she wrote the introduction to my first book of stories, and I owe her very much for that. We've been friends all these years (*CNVRS*, p. 81).

Elizabeth Bowen, as we have seen, was another older writer who befriended Eudora Welty. The two women had admired each other's work before they met in 1949, and they shared a profound appreciation of Virginia Woolf. Bowen's *Tatler* review of *Delta Wedding* was one of the most astute and appreciative assessments Welty's fiction received in the first decade of her career. Bowen observed that the two

extremes of Welty's achievement in her first three volumes
of fiction were an almost bald realism and a poetry capable
of 'flying particles of genius'. Her best work was balanced
between the two, and *Delta Wedding* exemplified it.

> There is a heart-breaking sweetness about this book,
> a sense of the momentum, joy, pain and mystery of
> life. DELTA WEDDING is not specifically American:
> I think it strikes a note to which people all over the
> world will respond. I should like to think that DELTA
> WEDDING may, in time, come to be recognised as a
> classic.[7]

What for Bowen is 'a heart-breaking sweetness' makes
one male American reviewer feel as if he has eaten a
barrel of molasses and sets others grumbling about the
flowery preciousness of the writing.[8] At least part of
Bowen's admiration derived from her understanding of
the almost Woolfian manipulation of point of view and
subtle revelation of interior life that Welty achieved in
the novel. Unlike many male critics who were impatient
with the novel's apparent lack of action, Bowen champions
a woman writer's use of the techniques of interiorisation
and radical slowing of time which had been used earlier by
Proust and Joyce. She does not even comment on Welty's
use of a domestic setting and feminine central consciousness
which many masculine readers, especially in America, find
trivial and dull. Instead she seems simply to assume that
these are important subjects for the novel.

Although distinctive traditions of women's writing and
the friendship of older writers like Porter and Bowen
provided precedents and encouragement, Welty was also
supported by men like John Rood of *Manuscript*, and
Robert Penn Warren and Cleanth Brooks of *The Southern
Review*. She has always seen her work within the wider
context of modern fiction undifferentiated by gender. While

male writers such as Chekhov, Forster and Faulkner were
important to her development, however, she used what she
learned from them in uniquely feminine contexts. As she
participated in the modernist projects of redefining heroism
and exploring sexuality, she offered feminine perspectives
that often differ radically from those of male writers.

In Welty's fiction, heroic behaviour occurs in a wide
variety of roles, male and female. Instead of the traditional
pattern of individual male subjectivity with its demands
for self-definition and domination, Welty pictures the
masculine hero from outside. Repeatedly she presents a
beloved male observed and indulged by a whole family,
especially by its women. He embodies a kind of joyous
phallic energy but is ultimately vulnerable and dependent
upon his connection with women. George Fairchild of *Delta
Wedding*, Jack Renfro of *Losing Battles*, Judge McKelva and
Phil Hand of *The Optimist's Daughter*, and Uncle Daniel of
The Ponder Heart are only the most obvious examples of
the type.

Many heroic women move through her pages. There
are fierce and demanding teachers like Miss Eckhart in
The Golden Apples and Miss Julia Mortimer whose spirit
dominates the rural world of *Losing Battles*, both seen
from various external points of view by their former
students. Strong mother figures as different as gentle Ellen
Fairchild of *Delta Wedding* and formidable Becky McKelva
of *The Optimist's Daughter* are balanced by headstrong but
admirable younger women like Virgie Rainey, the sturdy
orphan girl Easter of *The Golden Apples*, and Laurel Hand
of *The Optimist's Daughter*. Finally there are solitary female
figures who can be triumphant like the old woman of 'A
Worn Path' or comic, like the narrator of 'Why I Live at the
P.O.' or tragic, like Clytie of the story named for her.

In creating such characters Eudora Welty redefines
central motifs in the dominant tradition of American
fiction described by Leslie Fiedler in *Love and Death in the*

American Novel. The traditional American hero is a solitary white male like James Fenimore Cooper's Deerslayer or Herman Melville's Ishmael or Mark Twain's Huckleberry Finn, sharing an adventurous life outside the bounds of civilisation with a dark-skinned man who teaches him how to live in harmony with nature. The negative side of this Edenic vision is the fact that the hero's life is predicated upon a rejection of his proper human community and any ties with the feminine. The masculine American heroic tradition glorifies a pattern of infantile escapism and refuses artistically to engage the responsibilities of adult sexual and social relationships. Philip Fisher has recently argued in *Hard Facts* that the implications of this pattern go even deeper than mere escape. Fisher sees Cooper's Deerslayer novels as creating a cultural myth of innocence which masks or erases the facts of genocide and destruction of the landscape produced by European settlement of the North American continent.[9] Other critics like R. W. B. Lewis and Leo Marx have exposed similar contradictions in the pastoral myth of American innocence; Annette Kolodny has analysed the traditional description of the landscape as feminine and its exploitation as rape.[10]

Clearly the American novel has been preoccupied with issues that stand outside the main focus of the English novel. From its beginnings with Richardson's *Pamela*, the English novel has placed women and their domestic world at the centre of its concerns, and many of the great nineteenth-century English practitioners of the novel were women. Nancy Armstrong's *Desire and Domestic Fiction* makes a convincing case for the novel as the very embodiment and codifier of rising middle-class female power in English culture.[11] Eudora Welty's reliance on Austen, the Brontës, Woolf and Forster sets her in the English rather than the American tradition. To be sure, there were earlier women writers in her own country who presented alternative models for American fiction: novelists

like Willa Cather, Sarah Orne Jewett, Kate Chopin, Ellen
Glasgow, and Zora Neale Hurston, who concentrated on the
human community in the American landscape. All of them
saw human experience as closely tied to the land in harmony
with natural processes, and the lives of women were central
to their fiction. Thus their work stands in sharp contrast to
the 'heroic' masculine American tradition with its portrayal
of nature as an antagonist to be defeated, dominated, and
exploited. Eudora Welty should be seen as a member of
the distinguished company of these American women, who
created for herself a mode of fiction nourished by Anglo-
European precedent but also by American materials such
as the regional Southwest humour and traditional tall tale
of frontier days and the popular fiction by women writers
which has always outsold the masculine literature of 'high
seriousness'.

Nathaniel Hawthorne complained bitterly about the
large tribe of women 'scribblers' whose sentimental novels
were the overwhelming popular choice in his day. Leslie
Fiedler was the first American critic to accord serious value
to such works, turning away from the academic canon
of 'high literature' in the 1960s and 1970s to consider
the immense cultural impact of Harriet Beecher Stowe's
Uncle Tom's Cabin and Margaret Mitchell's *Gone With the
Wind*. Fiedler defines this domestic fiction by its emotional
appeals for social causes such as abolition and temperance,
and its support of a feminine, family-centred system of
values. Feminist critics Ann Douglas and Jane Tompkins
have followed Fiedler in reassessing this popular genre and
arguing that in many ways it is more central to American
culture than the tradition of the masculine heroic novel.[12]

Welty, as we have seen, abjures any didactic purpose for
literature, but her interest in the family and the feminine
perspective allies her with the long American tradition of
domestic fiction. While she concentrates upon a similar
range of subjects, she never falls into the sentimentality

and cliché of the domestic tradition, because – to use
Fiedler's terms – she trained herself in twentieth-century
modernism.

Like the other modernists, she explored sexuality, but
unlike most of them she approached it from the experience
of women. Her celebration of the erotic is dramatically different from James Joyce's bold dramatisation of Leopold's
and Molly Bloom's sexual fantasies and D. H. Lawrence's
depiction of physical love in works like *Women in Love*,
The Fox, and of course *Lady Chatterley's Lover*. While
these writers express masculine desire – even Joyce's Molly
Bloom is clearly a male-oriented portrait of female sexuality
– Welty's eroticism is centred in women's experience. It is
also less self-conscious and more discreet than Joyce's and
Lawrence's blazoning of female bodies and cataloguing of
sexual activities focused on male pleasure. Welty uses
characters such as the unapologetic Ruby Fisher of 'A
Piece of News', Virgie Rainey of *The Golden Apples*, and
Gloria Renfro of *Losing Battles* to present eroticism as a
simple, natural part of experience which women can enjoy
as autonomous beings, either inside or outside marriage.
The sensuous contentment of marriage is suggested in *Delta
Wedding* in scenes of amorous play like that between George
and Robbie Fairchild laughing and chasing each other in
the Yazoo River and then lying intertwined in a bed of
flowers and vines on the bank, or the simple picture of
newly-married Dabney Fairchild lying in the crook of her
husband's arm at a picnic.

Male philanderers like King MacLain of *The Golden
Apples* or the goatish Mr Don McInnis of 'Asphodel' or
the bigamist of 'Old Mr Marblehall' are all seen from an
indulgent comic distance. Their female victims are often
as comic as they are, and seem no more ruffled than hens
enduring the attentions of the local rooster. This kind
of presentation can trivialise male sexual predation, but
Welty either balances her acceptance of such behaviour

with similar freedom for her women characters, or else indicates the cost to the wronged women as in her tender portraits of King MacLain's wife and the bewildered and betrayed Jenny of 'At the Landing'.

Welty is sometimes charged with sentimentality, but attentive reading of her fiction reveals at least as many troubled relationships as satisfying ones. In the early story 'Flowers for Marjorie' an unemployed young husband is filled with rage by the complacent physical happiness of his pregnant wife and in a flash of sexual hatred murders her with a butcher knife. Memorable examples of failed marriages appear in her novels, notably in *Delta Wedding*, where the estrangement of a central married couple create tension and fear of disaster for the hopeful bride and groom. Even such a comic event as Uncle Daniel's accidental murder of his young wife Bonnie Dee in *The Ponder Heart* is ultimately grotesque and horrifying.

Yet Welty is very far indeed from the sexual disgust and despair of writers like Ernest Hemingway, William Faulkner and Saul Bellow, whose 'existential' heroes set a fashion for sexual bitterness and misogyny. These men come at the end of the American tradition of masculine escape, when the settled and increasingly urban life of twentieth-century America negates the fantasies that originated in the frontier experience. They seem unwilling to relinquish their archaic values and resentful of pressures to do so, pressures for which they blame female desire. Hemingway heroes like the hunters in 'The Short Happy Life of Francis Macomber' and 'The Snows of Kilimanjaro' project their own inadequacies on to women by treating them as treacherous or contemptible. In *The Sound and the Fury*, Faulkner uses characters like Quentin and Jason Compson to express despair and resentment of female sexuality in their behaviour toward their sister Caddy. In *The Bear* Isaac McCaslin's refusal to consider his wife's interests and his subsequent escape into wilderness solitude recapitulate the flight from the feminine into the idealised all-male world of adventure which is common to Melville, Cooper, and Twain. Even though Faulkner presents McCaslin's retreat ironically, there is no alternative model of heroic behaviour in his novels and stories, but instead a repetition of sexual horror and flight.

The recent work of feminist film critics on cinematic point of view, or 'the gaze' of the camera, sheds an interesting light on Welty's unusual ability to define her own creative space and express female sexuality positively in the broad tradition of the novel and within the more particular context of American fiction. Critic Ann Kaplan asks who looks at whom in films, and she answers that question with a description of the male gaze which has dominated the cinema from its origins. Kaplan bases her approach on the French psychoanalytic view informed by the work of Jacques Lacan, Julia Kristeva and others. These theorists assume that 'woman cannot enter the world of the symbolic, of language, because at the very moment of the acquisition of language, she learns that she lacks the phallus, the symbol that sets language going through a recognition of difference. . . .' Women's relation to language is necessarily negative because it is based on a lack. 'In patriarchal structures,' Kaplan explains, 'woman is located as other (enigma, mystery), and is thereby viewed as outside of (male) language.' As part of the patriarchal linguistic and semiotic system, the dominant (Hollywood) cinema presents narratives constructed according to masculine desire, in a phallocentric language that expresses the male unconscious. Women are eroticised and objectified in these narratives, forced by a power-dynamic of invasion and appropriation into a static and wordless posture. These tactics of domination and containment are justified by the standard Freudian arguments about male fear of the vagina and the overwhelming power of the mother.[13]

Kaplan does question the essential pessimism of the

psychoanalytic perspective and suggests that women can also employ the gaze. They can grant themselves the power of vision and definition of the world in narratives both cinematic and linguistic. Kaplan sees some hope in experimental studies unrelated to psychoanalytic theory, for they suggest that the formative experiences of looking occur in the mother–child relationship and offer instances of mutual gazing rather than the subject–object kind that reduces one person to submission.

If Ann Kaplan had examined Eudora Welty's fiction, she would have found a whole range of examples of a female gaze which creates mutual subjectivity and much emphasis upon the mother as central family influence. Welty describes the world primarily as women and children experience it, but her vision includes men as individualised subjects who may not be fully comprehensible to the observer but who are nevertheless accepted as fully human. The difference that makes them 'other' than the narrator creates mystery and possibility rather than resentment or defensive stereotyping. Once again George Fairchild and Troy Flavin of *Delta Wedding* come to mind, for they are the masculine objects of most attention in the novel. Both are heroic, sexually potent and outside the control of the women whose points of view constitute the narration. Yet each is also seen subjectively, in the sense that his personal vulnerabilities and needs are appreciated, and his individualism respected. King MacLain of *The Golden Apples*, who is often presented as almost the caricature of the lascivious satyr, is also seen sympathetically by Virgie Rainey when he becomes a grotesque old man. That young woman has just lost her mother, but rather than indulge her grief, she is attentive to both the selfishness and the defiant vitality of the old reprobate. Examples could be multiplied by the score, from Welty's many short stories as well as her novels.

If psychoanalysis provided an adequate account of human

psychology, it would be difficult to explain how Eudora Welty was able to envision and define a condition free of male struggles for domination. One wonders how women have ever succeeded in using language to express any distinctively feminine experience if linguistic competence requires even the symbolic possession of a phallus. In the terms of psychoanalytic film criticism, the appropriation of the gaze by women would be impossible. The novels of Austen, the Brontës, Eliot and Woolf would be mere permutations of patriarchal narratives. The feminine could exist in fiction *only* as a lack. Clearly such an argument is tautological. If we define the world as masculine, then we will of course discover that all cultural material is masculine, that women writers can produce only masculine language and imagery and that women characters are only negations.

Feminist critics who subscribe to a psychoanalytic approach unwittingly adopt the same patriarchal gaze they criticise. The Freudian argument that the phallus is the only sexual marker in human culture is one-sided and incomplete. It fails to acknowledge the longer and more widespread tradition of reverence for the female body as major signifier of power throughout Paleolithic and Neolithic civilisations and surviving even in the Bronze Age. Ann Kaplan begins to question the psychoanalytic tradition by calling attention to empirical studies of mothers and children, and that is a start. But feminist thinking has generally gone much further than that, assuming from Mary Wollstonecraft on down, that women's experience is at least as important as men's and that language is a human instrument (or game) that can be used (or played) by both sexes. Indeed English and French, among other languages, assume a female identity for language with expressions such as 'mother tongue' and '*langue maternelle*'. Some elements of language are undoubtedly skewed in the masculine direction, such as the generic use of the masculine for humankind, but the ability of women to speak and write their own experience is evident in an increasing flow of texts by women over the past four hundred years. Eudora Welty is a major contributor to their reorientation of literary language and vision, following such bold foremothers as Virginia Woolf in defining the feminine gaze.

Welty can be said to be deliberately displacing the phallic and Oedipal presumptions of patriarchal culture, of which Freudian psychoanalysis is but a part. Patricia Yaeger ingeniously demonstrates how Welty questions the signification of phallic imagery in 'Moon Lake', by placing it on the periphery of the very feminine milieu of a girls' summer camp. We will explore Yaeger's argument in greater detail in a later chapter, but for the present it is enough to note the affectionate but ironic and dismissive treatment of masculine narcissism in the following description of the one male at the camp – a Boy Scout lifeguard – as he is observed by two of the campers on a night after he has rescued another girl from drowning.

The Boy Scout, little old Loch Morrison, was undressing in his tent for the whole world to see. . . .

His candle – for that was all it was – jumping a little now, he stood there studying and touching his case of sunburn in a Kress mirror like theirs. He was naked and there was his little tickling thing hung on him like the last drop on the pitcher's lip. He ceased or exhausted study and came to the tent opening again and stood leaning on one raised arm, with his weight on one foot – just looking out into the night, which was clamorous.

It seemed to them he had little to do!

Hadn't he surely, just before they caught him, been pounding his chest with his fist? Bragging on himself? . . . His silly, brief, overriding little show they could well imagine there in his tent of separation in the middle

A GENEROUS COMIC MUSE

of the woods, in the night. Minnowy thing that matched his candle flame, naked as he was with that, he thought he shone forth too. Didn't he?

Nevertheless, standing there with the tent slanting over him and his arm knobby as it reached up and his head bent a little, he looked rather at loose ends.[14]

This indulgent portrait is consistent with Eudora Welty's treatment of men throughout her work. This passage acknowledges the boy's genuine bravery by placing the observing girls in an ironic position. They refuse to praise the heroic feat he performed earlier in the day, and they belittle what they imagine to be his masculine vanity. Yet at the same time, they are correct in describing his physical appearance as unimpressive and in noticing his own unheroic manner of indecision and wistful boredom. Even though Loch Morrison has performed the role of the hero, he remains an ordinary boy whose phallic body is far from awesome. Typically in Welty's fiction, masculine heroism and sexuality are seen in this kind of complex light – acknowledged and credited, but not given central place. The phallus is not the signifier of authority. For Welty, masculine energy seems only one of many necessary elements in the human community, while the unifying and steadying and supportive forces of community tend to be feminine.

Welty's use of myth even more radically displaces the cultural phallocentrism which since Freud has been identified especially with the story of Oedipus. In order to see the significance of Welty's mythic adaptations, it is necessary to understand the nature of Freud's investment in the Oedipus story. The pattern of struggle between father and son is inherited from much earlier materials – the Greek creation stories in which the father gods Uranos and Cronos are murdered by sons who usurp their power. In the story of Uranos and Cronos, the

crime is explicitly sexual, as the son Cronos castrates
his father. This pattern seems characteristic not only of
Greek culture but also of subsequent patriarchies. Thus
Freud seems to have intuitively fixed upon a narrative
of immense explanatory power when he chose the story
of Oedipus's murder of his father and marriage with his
mother to symbolise unconscious desires in the family.

Christine Froula and other feminist critics have docu-
mented a darker side to Freud's achievement, however.
Early in his career, in the 1880s, Freud began his work
with hysterical patients and developed his seduction theory
to account for the sexual abuse which his analysis revealed in
every case to have been suffered in the patient's childhood.
Almost always the sexual abuse came at the hands of a family
member, and more particularly, the father. By the end of the
century, however, Freud had abandoned seduction theory
and turned instead to the Oedipus myth from which he
developed the famous theory which concentrates on threats
to the father's power rather than on the abuse of that power
which seduction theory had revealed. Christine Froula cites
the work of Luce Irigaray, Alice Miller, Florence Rush and
other feminist critics of psychoanalysis in support of her
argument that Freud abandoned seduction theory because it
threatened patriarchal power and placed him in a powerless
position by reason of his role as confidant and explicator
of its female victims' plight. By developing the alternative
theory of the Oedipus complex, Freud was able to discredit
the accusations of the abused daughters of the patriarchy
and thus silence women's narratives of their marginalisation
and repression. Froula demonstrates that such a tactic is in
fact a very old one in European/American culture, which
Freud has recapitulated in a monolithic theoretical form.[15]
The narrative of Oedipus (the fathers) has been substituted
for the narrative of the mothers and the daughters.

Eudora Welty does not accept such an investment of
power in the masculine. Patricia Yaeger has shown how

Welty's relation to patriarchal discourse can be illuminated by Mikhail Bakhtin's view of language as 'a dynamic conversation' or dialogue between the individual writer and inherited literary traditions and ideologies. 'We remain in the midst of a revolution in discourse,' Yaeger argues, in which women writers discover their power to express their own circumstances in the 'covert but dialogic relation between dominant and muted speech'. Thus 'feminocentric writing will be not only in conflict but also in dialogue with the dominant ideologies it is trying to dislodge'.[16] Welty can be seen in this context as one who offers alternative mother-centred narratives in dialogue with those of the patriarchy. Phallic energy and male versions of heroism appear in her fiction, but they are displaced from their traditionally central position. By celebrating the power of the mother, the autonomous sexuality of daughters like Virgie Rainey and the profound use of female-centred myth, Welty's fiction contradicts traditional narrative discourse empowering the patriarchy. Instead of subscribing to Freudian theory, she turns to patterns of mythology which derive from pre-patriarchal culture and are concerned with feminine power.

Welty has said that her use of mythology is conscious. 'I've lived with mythology all my life. It is just as close to me as the landscape. It *naturally* occurs to me when I am writing fiction' (*CNVRS*, p. 224). Not long after finishing college she read the one-volume edition of Sir James Frazer's *The Golden Bough*, and it became a kind of bible for her, a reference she kept at her desk like her dictionary and Brewer's *Dictionary of Phrase and Fable*.[17] Frazer's emphasis on fertility rituals and his interpretation of the accompanying myths impressed her deeply, providing symbolic materials for much of her best writing in the 1940s. When she was introduced to the landscape of the Mississippi Delta, mythic associations came immediately to mind, especially the myth of Demeter and

Persephone, which she discussed in her correspondence as early as 1937. The ancient story of mother and daughter continued to fascinate her so profoundly that she wrote her first full-scale novel, *Delta Wedding*, as an exploration of its meaning for contemporary life in a war-torn world.[18] Welty employed this myth, as a later chapter will show, to depict a world based not on power struggles or on masculine sexual desire, but instead on the endlessly renewing cycles of fertility and rebirth, forces which support all life in harmony with the environment, rather than threatening it or trying to impose violent control. Welty's vision supports peace rather than war, cooperation rather than domination, and therefore comedy rather than tragedy.

As a stylist, Eudora Welty's most characteristic expression is lyrical and impressionistic, but always grounded in precise physical detail. She is a versatile prose writer, however, who can also write with the bare sort of realism we associate with masculine writers like Ernest Hemingway. At the other extreme she can employ an exotic, dreamlike fairytale mode which reminded some early reviewers of Isak Dinesen, or a flat caricature or grotesque similar to that used by other Southern writers such as William Faulkner, Carson McCullers, Tennessee Williams and Flannery O'Connor and labelled 'Southern gothic' by critics.

Welty's use of metaphor and simile is one of the most noticeable characteristics of her style. Edward Kessler criticises Welty's metaphors as being too domesticated, arguing that she uses comparisons that diminish objects and events around her characters in order to render the external world comfortable.[19] In fact, her range of metaphor is very broad and her use of analogy quite flexible. She may describe a sunset in *Delta Wedding* by saying, 'The sun went down lopsided and wide as a rose on a stem in the west, and the west was a milk-white edge, like the foam of the sea'; and say that 'the endless fields glowed like a hearth in firelight'. But the early story 'Clytie' ends with the following comic and terrible description of the main character's suicide: 'When Old Lethy found her, she had fallen into the barrel, with her poor ladylike black-stockinged legs up-ended and hung apart like a pair of tongs' (*CS*, p. 90). Sex is described as analogous to drowning in *Delta Wedding* (p. 254). And in one of the most lyrically transcendent passages in all her stories, she describes a kind of baptismal moonlight swim in *The Golden Apples*, taken by Virgie Rainey the night after her mother's funeral, with similes which open out and out into the universe.

> She felt the sand, grains intricate as little cogged wheels, minute shells of old seas, and the many dark ribbons of grass and mud touch her and leave her, like suggestions and withdrawals of some bondage that might have been dear, now dismembering and losing itself. She moved but like a cloud in skies, aware but only of the nebulous edges of her feeling and the vanishing opacity of her will, the carelessness for the water of the river through which her body had already passed as well as for what was ahead (*CS*, p. 440).

Mississippi is full of whimsical names which Eudora Welty has delighted in using all her writing life. The classical affectations of nineteenth-century Southern culture resulted in widespread use of antique Roman names such as Quintus, Marcus and Lucius, as well as names of gods and goddesses. These, combined with the inventiveness and illiteracy of folk culture, evolved in twentieth-century rural usage into many diminutive and filigreed forms. In the story 'Asphodel', maiden ladies are named Sabina and Phoebe; in 'The Winds' there is a character named Cornella, and the plantation world of *Delta Wedding* presents a servant named Partheny; the servant in *The Ponder Heart* is called Narciss and the servant in 'Clytie' is named Lethy. People are named for places, like the domestic named Missouri in

The Optimist's Daughter, or named according to relationship, like Little Uncle in *Delta Wedding* and Papa-Daddy
or Sister or Uncle Rondo in 'Why I Live at the P.O.'.
Welty has observed that her fellow Mississippians often
do not distinguish fiction from reality and therefore assume
that she takes all her characters from life. Once a woman
angrily threatened her in the local grocery store for using the
name Primrose, assuming that Miss Welty was describing a
relative. On the other hand, the name Virgie came from an
uneducated woman who was nursing a member of Welty's
family. When asked if she minded having her name used
in a story, the woman said, 'Why no, Hon, you go right
ahead.'[20]

A brief chronological survey of Eudora Welty's fiction
will demonstrate how she trained herself in a variety
of narrative and descriptive forms in her early stories,
and then explored the potential of specific techniques
more deeply as they were called forth by the particular
situations and thematic concerns of each subsequent
work. Her prose style varies according to the purpose
of each individual story as it begins to define itself in
the writing. 'Everything I write teaches me how to do
it as I go,' she explains (*CNVRS*, p. 244). Stylistically the
earliest stories, collected in *A Curtain of Green* (1941), are
remarkably different from each other, from the grotesque
comic dialogue of 'Petrified Man' and 'Why I Live at
the P.O.' to the acutely detailed realism of 'Death of a
Traveling Salesman' and the whimsical and gossipy tone
of the female chorus which narrates 'Old Mr Marblehall'.
Despite their differences, all are intricately constructed and
as precise in language and detail as poetry. Welty describes
the careful process of revising as analogous to the feminine
art of sewing. After typing a draft of a story, 'I revise with
scissors and pins. Pasting is too slow and you can't undo

it, but with pins you can move things from anywhere to anywhere, and that's what I really love doing – putting things in their best and proper place, revealing things at the time when they matter most' (*CNVRS*, p. 89). They must be read slowly and attentively. All of Eudora Welty's prose requires this kind of attention, and it is a quality her work shares with that of Joyce and Woolf.

Some of the stylistic techniques which Welty is teaching herself to use in the early stories collected in *A Curtain of Green* are regional dialect, the grotesque, and comic names. Later, in her mature work, they are used with more subtlety and restraint than at the early exuberant stage of discovery. Welty's uncanny ear for the distinctive rhythms and idioms of Southern speech is obvious in the opening passages of 'Petrified Man', a story presented almost entirely in dialogue and set in a beauty parlour.

> 'Reach in my purse and git me a cigarette without no powder in it if you kin, Mrs Fletcher, honey,' said Leota to her ten o'clock shampoo-and-set customer. 'I don't like no perfumed cigarettes.' (*CS*, p. 17).

This story is also typical in its comic use of the grotesque. The vulgarity of the beauty parlour is conveyed by colours – lavender walls, henna-dyed hair, women with scarlet lips and blood-red fingernails. The pivotal event concerns a freak show complete with a two-headed baby in a jar, Negro pygmies, and a supposedly petrified man who is in fact a disguised rapist.

'Why I Live at the P.O.' presents a cast of characters who might thrive in a freak show. There is a tap-dancing two-year-old girl named for Shirley Temple, a three-hundred-pound Mama, an intoxicated transvestite Uncle Rondo, wearing his niece's kimono and staggering out into the backyard to collapse upon an extravagantly bearded grandfather named Papa-Daddy, who is lying in a hammock. When an interviewer asked Welty about such exaggeration, she explained that she had used it early in her career because she had not yet learned more subtle methods for revealing character. 'In those early stories I'm sure I needed the device of what you call the "grotesque". That is, I hoped to differentiate characters by their physical qualities as a way of showing what they were like inside – it seemed to me then the most direct way to do it' (*CNVRS*, p. 84).

After the realistic and comic early stories of *A Curtain of Green*, *The Robber Bridegroom* (1942) represents a new departure. The second book is a fantastic novella relating events along the Natchez Trace of the Mississippi frontier as if they belonged in the collections of the brothers Grimm. The story's heroine is a lovely girl named Rosamond, with a wicked stepmother, a simple-minded father and a mysterious handsome lover. The classic fairytale plot is a frame which allows Welty to treat the violent habits of frontier life in a simplified language of wonder that renders them charming rather than horrifying.

In *The Wide Net* (1943), Welty began experimenting with a dreamlike lyricism which is often haunting but occasionally loses the reader in its vagueness. In an early review Diana Trilling complained that the style of the stories was precious and self-consciously dancelike, and Elizabeth Bowen wrote that one or two of the stories 'made me terrified that she might be headed for esoteric incomprehensibility.'[21] At the same time, however, Welty was exploring the relevance of folklore and mythology to realistic treatment of ordinary life and to the materials of history. In 'First Love', for instance, she imagines an almost magical aura surrounding the flamboyant Aaron Burr, convicted of treason in 1807 for plotting to deliver the United States into the hands of Britain. His conspiracies are witnessed by a deaf-mute boy to whom Burr and his accomplice seem marvellous beings from another world.

'The Wide Net' is a modern-day fertility ritual in a comic mode, with a young husband enlisting friends to help him drag a river for the body of his pregnant wife. He performs a kind of joyous underwater quest which results in nets full of fish and the recovery of his wife unharmed. Other stories, such as 'Livvie', 'Asphodel' and 'At the Landing', dramatise the intoxicating energy of sexuality as it affects the lives of various kinds of women, and Welty uses mythic allusions to suggest the vibrant magnetism of potent males. In these stories myth places ordinary events in the context of timeless life-forces.

Welty's first full-length novel, *Delta Wedding* (1946), is a profoundly serious exploration of the relation of myth to actual life. As she has recalled, she produced it without any plan at all, just writing the chapters as they came to her and sending them to her friend John Robinson in Italy.[22] In spite of her feeling that she wrote without a plan, the novel does have an impressionistic structure, with a series of rituals leading up to the wedding. She may have been completely unaware of the possibilities Virginia Woolf had revealed to her, but the impact of *To the Lighthouse* is evident in the way Welty was able to use fragmented point of view and focus on the mother in a large and complicated family. *Delta Wedding* represents her full discovery of the family as a microcosm of society and as a major subject for the rest of her career.

In *The Golden Apples* (1949), Welty continued to rely on a mythic substratum for symbolism. In this closely-related cycle of stories about several families in Morgana, Mississippi, the story of Zeus seducing Danae by taking the form of a shower of gold in her lap intertwines with allusions to the mischievous philanderings of Pan-like wood-gods and symbolic references to Yeats's 'Song of the Wandering Aengus'. The final story's meaning depends on the myth of Perseus and Medusa for a revelation of the interdependence of heroism and sacrifice in people's lives. It ends with the main character sitting on a graveyard fence in the rain, hearing 'the running of the horse and bear, the stroke of the leopard, the dragon's crusty slither, and the glimmer and the trumpet of the swan' (*CS*, p. 461).

The Ponder Heart (1956) is a comic novella narrated by an eccentric spinster hotelkeeper named Edna Earle Ponder. Her vision of her world is the real subject of the novella (*CNVRS*, p. 10). The name Edna Earle comes from a popular romantic novel from Welty's youth called *St Elmo* (*OWB*, p. 7), and 'Ponder' is a relatively common Mississippi name represented at least ten times in the Jackson telephone book. Welty chose the name for its comic effect and perhaps also for its punning suggestions of ponderousness for Uncle Daniel's exaggerated motivations of generosity. Another pun in the story is the physical enactment of the colloquial expression, 'Tickled to death to see you.' Bonnie Dee Peacock, Uncle Daniel's young wife, is literally tickled to death as her over-eager husband seeks to allay her fears during a thunderstorm. The story's climactic event is the zany murder trial which ensues.

Welty's third collection of short stories, *The Bride of Innisfallen* (1955), places familiar themes in European settings suggested by her own travels abroad. Marriage, the sensations of the traveller, and the tension between love and separateness, are particularly important in the title story and 'Going to Naples'. 'The Bride of Innisfallen' concerns the perceptions of a young bride travelling alone through Wales to Ireland by train and ferry. 'Going to Naples' is the story of a comic shipboard romance among Italian-American travellers to Naples. Much of Welty's energy in these two stories seems directed toward capturing the flavour of the foreign environment, and they seem to lack the authenticity and colour of her Mississippi fiction. 'Circe' represents a brief return to myth, as Welty tries to imagine herself in the place of Homer's immortal, 'condemned to live forever'.[23] 'The Burning' is a rather cryptic, surreal account of the burning of a plantation by Yankee soldiers during the Civil War.

With 'No Place for You, My Love' and 'Kin' sureness of control is restored in stories set in Louisiana and Mississippi of her own day. Welty has always attributed central power to place in fiction, and the stories in this collection illustrate her reliance on familiar settings for her best work.

Welty's second major novel, *Losing Battles* (1970), is a sustained experiment with a completely external point of view, rather than a reliance on describing the thoughts and motivations of her characters. 'I tried to see if I could make everything shown, brought forth, without benefit of the author's telling any more about what was going on inside the characters' minds and hearts' (*CNVRS*, p. 77). She feared that the novel might be overwritten, and indeed her elaborate similes are occasionally carried to excessive lengths. Like *Delta Wedding*, *Losing Battles* is a family novel that uses a central ritual as a device for bringing an extended family together and in the process revealing and resolving old antagonisms and problems. The Renfros of *Losing Battles* are poor white farmers living in the Mississippi hill country, as distinct from the upper-class Fairchilds of the Delta in the earlier work. 'I needed that region, that kind of country family, because I wanted that chorus of voices, everybody talking and carrying on at once. I wanted to try something completely vocal and dramatized,' she explains (*CNVRS*, p. 31). In this case the emphasis on fertility and renewal is carried by realistic events instead of the mythic allusion she had used in earlier works. Young Jack and Gloria Renfro renew their marriage when he returns from prison, community tensions are resolved at the boisterous picnic attended unexpectedly by the judge who had sentenced Jack to jail, and a serious drought is ended by a downpour of rain at the novel's conclusion. Behind the scenes as a motivating force is Miss Julia Mortimer, the spinster schoolteacher whose lifelong effort to educate and civilise the rural community is the source of the novel's title.

In her final novel, *The Optimist's Daughter* (1972),
Welty continues to explore family relationships as they are
revealed at ceremonial gatherings. Though the tone is still
comic and positive, the pivotal event this time is a death.
Social gatherings are occasioned by the resulting funeral,
and the real family reunion occurs only retrospectively
in the protagonist's consciousness as she returns to her
parents' house and reminisces about her father and mother,
both now dead. Welty fashions autobiographical materials
into a firm but gentle reflection on grief and the function
of memory. *The Optimist's Daughter* is not as lyrical as the
earlier novels; it is written in an altogether barer prose.
When poetry breaks through the restrained narration here,
however, it is perhaps even more affecting. One passage
near the end exemplifies both Welty's lyrical gift and her
lifelong faith in harmony and love. Laurel Hand wakes
after a night of grieving for her dead parents and also for
the young husband she lost in the war. She remembers a
happier time, when she and Phil were on a train bound for
their wedding in her Mississippi hometown.

When they were climbing the long approach to a bridge
after leaving Cairo, rising slowly higher until they rode
above the tops of bare trees, she looked down and saw
the pale light widening and the river bottoms opening
out, and then the water appearing, reflecting the low,
early sun. There were two rivers. Here was where they
came together. This was the confluence of the waters,
the Ohio and the Mississippi.

They were looking down from a great elevation
and all they saw was at the point of coming together,
the bare trees marching in from the horizon, the rivers
moving into one, and as he touched her arm she looked
up with him and saw the long, ragged, pencil-faint line
of birds within the crystal of the zenith, flying in a V
of their own, following the same course down. All they

could see was sky, water, birds, light, and confluence. It was the whole morning world. And they themselves were a part of the confluence. Their own joint act of faith had brought them here at the very moment, and matched its occurrence, and proceeded as it proceeded. Direction itself was made beautiful, momentous. They were riding as one with it, right up front. It's our turn! she'd thought exultantly. And we're going to live forever.[24]

3 Apprenticeship

Eudora Welty's perspective on the variety of Mississippi life she encountered as a WPA publicity agent was intimate and sympathetic. It is unusual for a writer to leave a visual record of such a formative period, but she has done so with the hundreds of photographs she took as she travelled around her state. These provide concrete, fixed evidence of her gaze as a young woman. We must of course distinguish between the medium of the photograph and that of the written word; the camera can only capture external images of the moment, while language can explore inner psychological states, complex actions and the passage of time. Nevertheless, Welty's photographs provide a unique definition of her concerns and the frame of her vision as an observer, the vision she would develop as she taught herself the craft of fiction. *A Curtain of Green* and *The Wide Net* explore the interests expressed by the photographs, in ways possible only with the written word.

The Depression period of the 1930s saw perhaps the greatest achievements in American documentary photography, with classic collections such as those in Erskine Caldwell's and Margaret Bourke-White's *You Have Seen Their Faces*, Dorothea Lange and Paul Taylor's *An American Exodus*, Richard Wright and Edwin Rosskam's *12 Million Black Voices* and James Agee's and Walker Evans' *Let Us Now Praise Famous Men*.[1] Most of these publications aimed to stimulate reform by making the nation vividly aware of widespread poverty. The photographs in these collections therefore presented images of filth, hunger, delapidated housing, and human despair.

Welty's pictures are strikingly different from these

documentaries of squalor and humiliation, just as they are different from the opposite extreme represented by Julia Peterkin's and Doris Ulmann's sentimental apology for the Old South, *Roll Jordon, Roll*, full of 'picturesque' images of 'happy darkies'.[2] The experience of travelling through the eighty-two counties of Mississippi taught Welty how protected her life had been, but rather than seeing poor blacks and whites as sociological data or political victims, she approached them with a sense of kinship and admiration for the spirit with which they lived their difficult lives. She remembers that the Depression made few noticeable changes in a state that was already the poorest in the nation, and she had no interest in making any political point.

Whatever you might think of those lives as symbols of a bad time, the human beings who were living them thought a good deal more of them than that. If I took picture after picture out of simple high spirits and the joy of being alive, the way I began, I can add that in my subjects I met often with the same high spirits, the same joy. Trouble, even to the point of disaster, has its pale, and these defiant things of the spirit repeatedly go beyond it, joy the same as courage.[3]

The majority of the photos are pictures of black Mississippians, and Welty's position as a shy white woman allowed her glimpses into their lives which no white man could have had. White men enforced a racial hierarchy which they exploited sexually as well as politically and economically. Since colonial times they had violated their professed allegiance to racial purity by widespread miscegenation outside marriage. The exercise of their power included sexual exploitation of black women, sexual humiliation of black men, violent punishment of insubordination, and careful segregation of white women from knowledge of these arrangements. Blacks were keenly

aware of the constant danger they faced under this system,
and Richard Wright testifies to the dual reality of which
most whites knew only one side. 'They have painted one
picture: charming, idyllic, romantic; but we live another:
full of fear of the Lords of the Land, bowing and grinning
when we meet white faces. . . .'[4] Eudora Welty's upbring-
ing had protected her from any detailed knowledge of these
matters, but she was too acute an observer not to have
glimpsed the hidden violence beneath the gracious surface
of Mississippi life. She would allude to these problems later
in her writing, but she remained a Southern lady who would
always be outside the lives of the people whom she met
and photographed. Her sex, her class, and her manner
worked to her advantage as a photographer, however. As a
woman, she was clearly removed from the sphere of white
male authority, and she represented no sexual threat. As a
young, gentle, and shy person, she seems as well to have
been able to put her black subjects at their ease. Because
she was white, they were required by the racial code to
cooperate with her, but because she was female and shy,
they had nothing to fear.

In her selection of both black and white subjects and in
her photographic technique, Welty is distinctively different
from most of the documentary photographers of the 1930s.
Walker Evans is perhaps the most famous of them, and his
photographs in *Let Us Now Praise Famous Men* are the most
artful attempts to emphasise the bareness and stark poverty
of poor sharecropping farmers' lives. Evans's frontal poses
and direct lighting sharply etch the stubble of beard on
the men's thin faces, the safety pins holding together the
deeply soiled and sacklike dresses of women and girls, and
the blank or tired or wary expressions in the eyes of all his
people.

Welty's subjects are usually very poor and often ragged,
living in the same kind of wooden shacks that Evans photographed, but she captures the basic human courage and

grace beneath the superficial badges of class and race. 'Boy
with his Kite' is almost a frontal pose, similar to those characteristic of Evans's work, but Welty caught the moment
at which the boy held up his homemade toy, looking at it
with a determined pride, rather than at the camera. The
smudges and holes in his sweater or the uneven length and
dusty look of his knickers are unimportant in comparison
to his achievement. In other pictures, many of mothers
and children, smiles and animated gestures similarly over-
shadow signs of poverty. In one, entitled 'Coke', a big
sister or young mother balances a baby on her knee as
she balances herself on her other foot and stands leaning
against the porch wall with her free hand resting, Coca-Cola
in hand, on a windowsill. Her sacklike dress has slipped
from one shoulder, and a ragged edge is noticeable on one
side of her hem, but the main impression of the image is
a jaunty relaxation expressed by the graceful alignment of
the girl's limbs with the baby's. In the picture of mother
and child entitled 'To Find Plums', there is harmony in
the pose of the smiling mother holding her daughter in her
arms, both in dresses and bright hats, facing the same way
in anticipation perhaps of the fruit they will find, mother
with a large bucket and daughter with her own miniature
made from a coffee tin (*OTOP*, pp. 29, 30, 47).

Welty used her privileged position as an unobtrusive
female observer to explore many of the same themes in
the lives of blacks which she would later dramatise in
her fiction: domestic life, women with children, courtship,
children's games, feminine rituals of work and recreation,
strong independent women in the community, and the overall comedy of manners which makes her fiction sometimes
reminiscent of her favourite, Jane Austen's.

One of the most memorable photographic images is
that of an old woman standing in her buttoned sweater
and hat and looking straight into the camera. In 1971
when she made her selection for *One Time, One Place*,

Welty was so struck by this picture that she made it her frontispiece.

> When a heroic face like that . . . looks back at me from her picture, what I respond to now, just as I did the first time, is not the Depression, not the Black, not the South, not even the perennially sorry state of the whole world, but the story of her life in her face. . . . Her face to me is full of meaning more truthful and more terrible and, I think, more noble than any generalization about people could have prepared me for or could describe for me now (*OTOP*, p. 7).

Other pictures of lone female figures include the figure of a young woman silhouetted against the sky with her hoe arrested in the air, as a graceful symbol of the intense labour exacted by cotton cultivation. Pictures of women working alone include one of a woman tending a boiling pot, another of a woman tending a cane press, and another of a washerwoman sitting in determined rest on her front steps as the wash dries on a line in the background. Independent professional women include a nurse standing before her house in her uniform, ready to leave for the day's work, a formidable schoolteacher on a Friday afternoon standing with hand on hip in immaculately starched and stylish clothes beside her suitcase while waiting for her ride or bus, a solemn fortuneteller with cards outspread, and a playful lady bootlegger with ice-pick raised in mock attack (*OTOP*, pp. 11, 14, 16, 19, 22, 23, 64–5). The photographs of solitary female figures establish an overall image of competent, determined independence.

Many other photographs capture the domestic world of women and children, while others are images of women together in town, shopping or standing with arms affectionately intertwined as they gaze up at the lighted signs and rides of the county fair they are about to enter. A number of pictures celebrate the bond of mother and child, some as solemn portraits, some as laughing moments of affection, and a number of pictures show children at play.

Another series of pictures provides a profound commentary on women's spiritual strength in the black community. Three pictures of Sunday activities in a Holiness church feature white-robed women in tableau-like poses with back-light flooding into the time exposure in a halo effect (*OTOP*, pp. 82–3, 86). One remarkable image presents a woman in white with veils flowing down over her shoulders. The woman closest to the camera almost fills the lower half of the picture, while above her on her right another woman, similarly robed, gazes into the camera, and just above her a third holds large cymbals poised on either side of her head. Behind the two large figures that dominate the foreground, the preacher stands with his Bible in hand, his face almost obliterated in shadow. The women are enormous, dazzling presences who dwarf the faint image of the preacher.

Welty described her visit to this church at some length in a 1945 *Vogue* article, emphasising the remarkable dominance of this shrivelled little preacher in his congregation. Apparently all money collected during the services was given to him, and he was the centre of absolute devotion for his largely female flock.[5] Yet the photograph in which he appears removes him from the centre of attention, and concentrates power in the hieratic white-robed figures of his deaconesses. Such an image prefigures the similar ways beloved males become the objects of adoration in Welty's novels but in a world seen from a woman's point of view. George Fairchild serves such a function in *Delta Wedding*, Uncle Daniel Ponder does in *The Ponder Heart*, Judge McKelva is the centre of attention for much of *The Optimist's Daughter*, and Jack Renfro is doted upon by all the women in *Losing Battles*. In each of these fictions, men are seen through the eyes of women, and stability and authority are fixed in women's relationships and rituals.

As Welty learned with her camera how to wait for the moment of revelation before clicking the shutter, she was also learning that only words could offer the medium for 'a fuller awareness of what I needed to find out about people and their lives.' Writing stories was the natural extension of the gaze of the camera, a way 'to part a curtain, that invisible shadow that falls between people, the veil of indifference to each other's presence, each other's wonder, each other's human plight' (*OTOP*, p. 8). After her WPA job ended in 1936 and she began publishing fiction, she put her camera away. For the rest of her life, she would explore the human comedy with the more discursive and narrative medium of language. All her fiction, however, would be affected by the visual lessons she had learned from photography and would adapt the sympathetic gaze that characterises her pictures to more complex narrative purposes.

If we read *A Curtain of Green* with the understanding that these first successful stories came out of the same period of apprenticeship in the 1930s as the photographs, we see how Welty attempted to imagine what lay beyond the visual surfaces of her fellow Mississippians' lives. An obvious example is 'Keela, the Outcast Indian Maiden', in which the grotesque and fantastic phenomenon of a circus Geek is explored in human terms.

One of the few public entertainments in the rural South was the travelling circus, generally a shabby affair offering human spectacles as well as a rather flea-bitten array of exotic animals to naive audiences. The perennial favourites of poor Southern townsfolk and farmers were not the standard acrobats or jugglers or trapeze artists or lion tamers, but human grotesques such as The Fat Lady, The Two-headed Baby, The Hermaphrodite, The World's Smallest Man and The Geek. The Geek was one of the more active and troubling spectacles among these freaks, for he represented a human being who had sunk into bestiality expressed by growling, gibbering, and eating small animals like chickens and rats alive.

In 'Keela, the Outcast Indian Maiden' Welty characterises the Geek as a scapegoat or 'Other' upon whom the dominant group – the 'civilised' citizens – can project its own fears about loss of control and human identity. She has made a complex statement about how the process works, by identifying this scapegoat with marginal ethnic groups – blacks and red Indians – and with the feminine. The Geek in the story was supposed to have been an ostracised Indian girl, and thus it appeared in its cage in a filthy red dress. In a society that supposedly idolised the 'lady' as the American South professed to do, such treatment of a young woman is strange indeed. The purpose of the story is to reveal the true identity of the 'Indian maiden' as that of a diminutive crippled black man who watches with glee as one white man insists on telling another white man how the imposture was exposed and the little black man was freed to return to his family. That a black male could have been kidnapped and humiliated in such a way reveals much about power relations in Southern society at the time. Even when a former circus employee seeks to find Little Lee Roy and atone in some way for the injustice done to him, the white man never addresses a word to the black man but instead tells the story to another white man. Thus the victim never is allowed to voice his own consciousness or to explain how the experience felt to him. He is denied subjectivity in a world controlled by white men. The final irony of the story is that after the white men have left, Little Lee Roy's children refuse to listen to his recital of their visit.

The circumstances in 'Keela, the Outcast Indian Maiden' strain credibility, and the device of having a conscience-tormented young man force his story upon a cynical tavern-operator while the object of the tale looks on does not seem very plausible. Yet the basic story was true; Welty heard it from a man who was building a booth at a county fair during her WPA travels. As she told an interviewer in 1942, 'I guess if you read it you must have known that it was true and not made up – it was too horrible to make up'. 'Keela' was her attempt to explore 'how people could put up with such a thing and how they would react to it' (*CNVRS*, pp. 5, 157). At the same time she was very subtly commenting upon the symbolic place of women and racial minorities in Southern life.

'A Worn Path' dramatises the kind of life that might lie behind the image of the heroic old woman in the photograph at the beginning of *One Time, One Place*. The story originated in the glimpse of a woman Welty saw while spending the day out in the country with a painter friend who was doing a landscape.

> I was reading under a tree, and just looking up saw this small, distant figure come out of the woods and move across the whole breadth of my vision and disappear into the woods on the other side. And . . . I knew she was going somewhere. I knew that she was bent on an errand, even at that distance. It was not casual. It was a purposeful, measured journey that she was making. And what I felt was – of course, that was my imagination I suppose, since I never knew – was that you wouldn't go on an errand like that, so purposefully, unless it were for someone else, you know. Unless it *were* like an emergency. And so I made it into a story by making it the one you'd be most likely to go for – a child (*CNVRS*, pp. 167–8).

Such inferences clearly derive from women's traditional roles as guardians and nurturers of children, and they define a distinctively feminine kind of heroism. Phoenix Jackson, the central character of 'A Worn Path', is fixed upon the need to keep her grandson alive. Even as a very old woman she is determined to spend an entire day plodding steadily through woods and fields toward town and the hospital where she can get the medicine he must have. Such motivation is not typical of the male hero, who is usually concerned with self-definition, as in the quest-motif of the courtly romance tradition and American versions like *Huckleberry Finn*, or with battles for dominance, as in classic warrior tales such as *Beowulf* and *The Iliad* and more recent adaptations such as the American western or police drama.

The major obstacle the old black woman encounters on her journey is the potentially heroic male figure of a hunter whom she meets on her journey. Phoenix Jackson has stumbled and fallen into the ditch beside the road, and the hunter helps her out. But then he questions her and tells her to go home. By placing the figure of an armed and physically vigorous male beside the frail old lady who refuses to be intimidated by his questions or the gun he aims at her, Welty dramatises the power of patience and determination. It is as if she is challenging the Southern male attachment to blood sports as means of proving virtue and strength. The tiny, elderly black woman in one brief story stands as an understated feminine alternative to the whiskey-drinking heroes of *The Bear*, William Faulkner's famous tale of masculine initiation to hunting in the Mississippi woods.

Other stories such as 'The Whistle' hypothesise the experiences of poor whites from glimpses Welty had of their lives. While visiting a friend in the countryside one spring, she was awakened late at night by a terrible whistle. She asked her friend what had happened and was told that the whistle was an alarm to warn of a freeze that could kill the young tomato plants in the fields. The country people would wake and cover their plants with whatever they had. In the morning, Welty and her friend could see the results. Clothing, bedding and old croker sacks were spread all over

the gardens. 'That just killed me,' Welty says, and the shock
of such poverty and sacrifice stimulated her to write the
story.[6] The action is centred on the consciousness of a
middle-aged woman sleeping beside her husband on the
floor of their wooden shack, cold to the bone under flimsy
bedclothes. Fatigue and chill keep her awake every night,
and only fantasies of hot weather and the tomato harvest
finally lull her into unconsciousness. On this night she is
jolted awake by the shrill whistle of the alarm, and she
and her husband must bare their own bed to cover the
beds of the plants that are their livelihood. Welty gives
the apparent defeat of the story's action an unexpected twist
by having the husband defiantly make a bonfire of the few
sticks of furniture in the cabin. He turns disaster into a
momentary burst of celebration and warmth which will of
course leave himself and his wife more destitute than ever,
once it has burned out.

Most of the stories in *A Curtain of Green* concern subjects
closer to Welty's own experience of Mississippi town-life
and take place in a feminine milieu. Central characters
range from young girls to mature women, and Welty uses
a variety of narrative approaches to render them.

'A Visit of Charity' and 'A Memory' present two
different girls' horrified perceptions of older women.
In 'A Visit of Charity' a young Campfire Girl (similar
to a Girl Scout) encounters what seems to her a witches'
den when she makes a visit to the Old Ladies' Home of
her town in order to win points in her club. Welty slyly
echoes fairytales such as Little Red Riding Hood, Hansel
and Gretel and Snow White in order to give the story
an uncanny atmosphere. The Campfire Girl looks like a
character from a fairytale as she jumps off her bus: 'She
wore a red coat, and her straight yellow hair was hanging
loose from the pointed white cap. . . .' The Old Ladies'
Home looks 'like a block of ice', and once inside she is
ushered into a room with two old crones, one of whom has

drawn her in with hands like bird claws. 'It was like being
caught in a robbers' cave, just before one was murdered.'
The girl's nervous visit captures the weirdness of old age
in the eyes of the young, who escape from its presence as
quickly as the Campfire Girl does, back into the heedless
world of normal life. We last see her safe on a bus again,
taking a big bite out of an apple.

In 'A Memory' a precociously sensitive adolescent girl
observes the vulgar antics of a man, a woman and two children on a local beach. Through the frame of her fingers,
as though through a secret window, she watches this rough
and overweight family in faded bathing suits insult, pinch
and tumble over each other in the sand. Her thoughts about
their untidy physical reality intertwine with her fantasies
about the boy in her school who is the object of her first
infatuation. The safety of her detachment and the haven
of her fantasies are gradually eroded as she becomes more
and more fascinated by the grotesque bodies and actions
of the family. The woman is the centre of the group, and
her body assumes monstrous proportions.

> Fat hung upon her upper arms like an arrested earthslide
> on a hill. With the first motion she might make, I was
> afraid that she would slide down upon herself into a
> terrifying heap. Her breasts hung heavy and widening
> like pears into her bathing suit. Her legs lay prone
> one on the other like shadowed bulwarks, uneven and
> distorted, upon which, from the man's hand, the sand
> piled higher like the teasing threat of oblivion (*CS*,
> p. 78).

Then the man pours sand down the woman's bathing
suit and the whole group laughs. The woman's body is
associated with enormous features on the landscape, but
rather than providing a secure sense of solidity, it seems
surrealistically fluid and ready to collapse. The climax of

the scene comes as the narrator looks up to see the woman
standing opposite the smiling man.

> She bent over and in a condescending way pulled down
> the front of her bathing suit, turning it outward, so that
> the lumps of mashed and folded sand came emptying out.
> I felt a peak of horror, as though her breasts themselves
> had turned to sand, as though they were of no importance
> at all and she did not care (CS, p. 79).

The unapologetic physicality of these ugly, boisterous
people invades the observing girl's complacency and suggests that protective, familiar boundaries can collapse at
any moment. The solidity of form is represented by the
monumental female shape which recalls the grotesquely
exaggerated votive figurines, popularly called 'Venuses', of
Paleolithic and Neolithic cultures. However, the narrator
feels nothing but revulsion and fear when she gazes at the
woman's body in the sand. When her breasts appear to
pour out of the bathing suit in mashed and distorted sandy
lumps, it is as if a whole physical reality which the man and
woman have made together – and an obviously sexual one –
can be casually dissolved. After the strangers have left, the
girl feels victimised 'by the sight of the unfinished bulwark
where they had piled and shaped the wet sand around their
bodies, which changed the appearance of the beach like the
ravages of a storm' (CS, p. 79).

If 'A Memory' expresses a horror of female sexuality,
'A Piece of News' presents a candid acceptance of sensual
pleasure that is much more typical of Welty's fiction and will
appear again and again in later works. This is a simple study
of a poor white woman during a rainy afternoon when she is
alone in her cabin after an assignation with a travelling coffee
salesman. Her husband Clyde, a grizzled moonshiner, has
been out working his still all day, and she has 'hitchhiked'
with a passing stranger, as she sometimes does when Clyde

'makes her blue'. The story begins on her return to the cabin, as she unwraps the sack of coffee the salesman has given her for her favours, and then lounges on the floor before the fire to dry herself. Ruby Fisher simply enjoys her body and stretches dreamily like a cat in the warmth before the fireplace. She is unapologetic about her sexual adventures, but when she reads on a scrap of newspaper that another Ruby Fisher has been shot by her husband, she teases herself with fantasies about how Clyde might have taken vengeance on her. When Clyde returns to the cabin, however, he only chides her briefly and then eats his supper. By indirection, the story defines an autonomous female sexuality that has only an oblique relation to patriarchal institutions defining traditional bonds between women and men. Ruby Fisher is able to pleasure herself without endangering her relationship to her husband.

One of the strangest stories in the collection is the title story, 'A Curtain of Green', in which the feminine setting of a flower garden is used to explore the interrelation of fertility and death. The main character is a newly-widowed woman who sequesters herself in her garden after her husband is killed by a falling tree. The only townsfolk who are mentioned, besides Mrs Larkin and her Negro gardener Jamie, are the neighbour women who sit in the windows of their houses waiting for rain in the afternoons and watching Mrs Larkin. It is these women's perspective on her obsessive gardening which opens the story, although point of view shifts to Mrs Larkin by the end.

Mrs Larkin appears to her neighbours to be 'over-vigorous, disreputable, and heedless' as she works in her old pair of men's overalls among her riotous plants. Her overalls have turned the colour of plants, and she seems to be submerging herself deliberately in the same vegetative forces that killed her husband. 'To a certain extent, she seemed not to seek for order, but to allow an over-flowering, as if she consciously ventured forever a little farther, a

little deeper, into her life in the garden' (*CS*, p. 108).
She has never directly expressed her grief over the loss
of her husband, but it rises to a climax of urgency on one
afternoon in the white heat before the daily rainstorm. She
raises her hoe above Jamie's back and thinks of taking out
her frustrations on his docile and vulnerable form.

> Such a head she could strike off, intentionally, so deeply
> did she know, from the effect of a man's danger and
> death, its cause in oblivion; and so helpless was she,
> too helpless to defy the workings of accident, of life and
> death, of unaccountability. . . . Was it not possible to
> compensate? to punish? to protest (*CS*, p. 111)?

Suddenly the rain begins to fall, her anger and grief
dissolve in tenderness and she collapses in a faint among
the flowers.

A far less satisfactory explosion of pent-up feeling
is the climactic event of 'Clytie'. This story is a study
of entrapment in a grotesquely comic form. It follows
the events in a decadent aristocratic family leading up
to the suicide of one of its members, a shy spinster who
is bullied and exploited by her older sister and drunken
brother. To outside observers, Miss Clytie looks ridiculous.
Welty describes her behaviour in town during a rainstorm
in comic terms which nevertheless also convey sympathy:

> The old maid did not look around, but clenched her
> hands and drew them up under her armpits, and sticking
> out her elbows like hen wings, she ran out of the street,
> her poor hat creaking and beating about her ears (*CS*,
> p. 82).

Most of the story is narrated from a perspective much
closer to Miss Clytie's own thoughts, and when she is
seen subjectively she is a sensitive observer of other

people. Oppressed by her sister and brother, she longs to know the mysteries of other lives and to have some genuine connection with them. But she grows more and more timid as she remains cut off from the townspeople and trapped in her own family's decaying mansion.

One day when the town barber comes to shave her invalid father, Clytie's curiosity overcomes her. 'Clytie came up to the barber and stopped. Instead of telling him that he might go in and shave her father, she put out her hand and with breathtaking gentleness touched the side of his face.' After a moment of stunned silence, both scream and retreat in opposite directions. In despair Clytie drowns herself in the rain barrel.

Three of Eudora Welty's best-known stories in *A Curtain of Green* share a vivid dramatic immediacy based on regional dialect. 'Petrified Man', 'Why I Live at the P.O.' and 'Lily Daw and the Three Ladies' are all set in feminine enclaves of small towns. Dialogue among characters is the basic form of the stories, with minimal narration from outside the action. 'Lily Daw and the Three Ladies' presents the comic efforts of a group of ladies to save the virtue of the young half-wit Lily Daw, who is being courted by the deaf xylophone player of a travelling show that has visited the town. 'Why I Live at the P.O.' is a *tour de force* of first-person narration in which an unmarried young postmistress recounts the zany events in her peculiar family on the Fourth of July which led her to snatch up the electric fan, a radio, an embroidered pillow, and an ironing-board and move into the Post Office to live. The most complex of these three stories, however, is 'Petrified Man', and it stands as the fullest example among these stories of Welty's comic gift with dialogue.

'Petrified Man' is a story not often discussed seriously by critics, but it is familiar because Welty has read it aloud to many audiences. Caedmon Records produced a recording of her reading that brings to life all the magic of the sound of Southern speech which readers may miss

on the page. In this story Welty manipulates the idioms of
banal conversation to satirise the triviality but also to reveal
the darker undercurrents of ordinary women's lives.

The story's setting in a beauty parlour allows for close
examination of a female society devoted to rituals designed
to arrest the destructive passage of time. Welty describes
it as a 'den of curling fluid and henna packs' in which
customers are 'gratified' in booths separated by lavender
swinging doors. The 'permanents' these ladies receive are
anything but lasting or salutary. Mrs Fletcher, for example,
the customer who is one of the two main characters, blames
her falling hair on the way her beautician Leota 'cooked' her
in the hair dryer after a previous permanent. Nevertheless,
the beauty parlour is a comic temple of female power where
women come for comfort and reassurance. One customer
even insisted on stopping in for a shampoo and set on the
way to the hospital to have a baby. ' "Just wanted to look
pretty while she was havin' her baby, is all," said Leota
airily. "Course, we was glad to give the lady what she was
after – that's our motto – but I bet a hour later she wasn't
payin' no mind to them little end curls" ' (CS, p. 24).

Leota's hardened perspective defines the underlying
problem which the story dramatises in two episodes of
Mrs Fletcher's weekly visits to the beauty parlour. Women
may try to control their bodies and preserve their looks,
but men inevitably involve them in the physical distortions
and pain of pregnancy. 'Petrified Man' is at its heart a story
about rape.

Each of the main characters assumes that she controls
her husband and is mistress of her fate, but each woman's
confidence is mistaken. Mrs Fletcher is uneasily pregnant
for the first time and says she is tempted not to have the
baby. When Leota suggests that her husband might beat
her on the head if she didn't, Mrs Fletcher haughtily asserts
that 'Mr Fletcher can't do a thing with me.' Leota winks
knowingly at herself in the mirror, thinking obviously of

how Mrs Fletcher got pregnant in the first place. Leota is overconfident about her own husband Fred, who is unemployed and spends his time fishing and drinking beer. She thinks he will obey her orders to go and find work in another town, but instead he finds an excuse to postpone such exertion.

The shocking central event of the story, which happens offstage and is reported by Leota to Mrs Fletcher when she returns for a second appointment, symbolically underscores these women's vulnerability to the basic male threat of sexual attack which lurks just outside the bounds of their comfortable lives. During Mrs Fletcher's first appointment in the story, Leota has raved about her new friend Mrs Pike. This woman is unusually observant and has guessed Mrs Fletcher's pregnant condition before it has been made public. In the second part of the story, Mrs Fletcher learns that Leota has turned against her new friend. Mrs Pike has used her perspicacity to see through the disguise of the 'Petrified Man' she and Leota observed at a travelling freak show. The man is a fugitive rapist from California, with a price of five hundred dollars on his head, and Mrs Pike has recognised his photograph in a crime magazine owned by Leota. Mrs Pike wins the reward and Leota is jealous.

The revelation of Leota's pettiness and the superficiality of her regard for Mrs Pike are minor points compared to the danger represented by the fraud in the freak show. A man who seemed safe to the point of petrifaction, and whom Mr and Mrs Pike had known as a benign neighbour in New Orleans, has assaulted at least four women in the past and could easily continue his predations if he were to remain at large. The story suggests that women in apparently civilised and peaceful communities cannot know which men they encounter casually may be capable of sexual violence against them. Mrs Pike is able to cause the rapist's capture, but the renegade element of male hostility represented by the Pikes'

little boy remains free to taunt the ladies in the final words of
the story and to suggest that he may grow up to be another
dangerous man.

Unexpected masculine hostility and violence is the climax
of 'Flowers for Marjorie', a story about an unemployed
young Southerner in New York, whose inadequacy in the
presence of feminine completeness leads him to murder
his wife. The young husband returns to his apartment
after a demoralising day out looking for work and finds
his wife Marjorie peacefully sitting by the window. Her
very presence seems to reproach him, with her warmth
and tenderness and her cloverlike fragrance.

> Her fullness seemed never to have touched his body.
> Away at his distance, backed against the wall, he regarded
> her world of sureness and fruitfulness and comfort, grown
> forever apart, safe and hopeful in pregnancy, as if he
> thought it strange that this world too, should not suffer
> (CS, p. 101).

He is suddenly filled with hatred at her inquiring 'out
of her safety into his hunger and weakness' and he snatches
a butcher knife and thrusts it under her breast. When he
leaves the apartment in a daze after the murder, he notices
portraits of the Virgin Mary along his way and graffiti in
the subway repeating 'God sees me, God sees me, God sees
me, God sees me'. Finally he tells a policeman that there
is a dead woman in his apartment, and the policeman
understands the childish helplessness of the young man.
' "Don't be afraid, big boy. I'll go up with you," he said'
(CS, p. 106).

In the much-anthologised 'Death of a Traveling Salesman', the spectacle of completeness in a pregnant woman
leads to an opposite conclusion. A lonely salesman's heart
literally bursts with longing to share the peace and harmony
he finds in the shack of a poor white couple who have taken

him in and fed him after his car accidentally ran off the road. He dies, stumbling toward his car in the middle of the night, ashamed to have been trespassing upon a fullness of life he cannot share.

As we have seen, mythology and folklore have been an intimate part of Eudora Welty's life since childhood. 'I have used not only Mississippi folklore but Greek and Roman myths or anything else, Irish stories, anything else that happens to come in handy that I think is an expression of something that I see around me in life' (*CNVRS*, pp. 107–108). She takes the long view of literary culture which assumes the validity of very old imaginative forms. *A Curtain of Green* includes a few experiments with techniques drawn from fairytale, and *The Robber Bridegroom* is an attempt to combine a number of fairytale motifs in a lighthearted tale of the Mississippi frontier. The heart of the story is in fact a traditional fairytale about the kidnapping of a beautiful maiden by a romantic robber on the Natchez Trace, combined with the basic idea of the story of Cupid and Psyche. Not until *The Wide Net*, however, did Welty attempt a serious and sustained intermingling of myth and folktale motifs with subjects that are essentially realistic.

Undoubtedly it was E. M. Forster's short stories that showed her how to dramatise the interpenetration of ordinary modern reality by mythic forces. In *The Celestial Omnibus* Forster injects the presence of the wood-god Pan into a stodgy picnic ('The Story of a Panic'), he pictures magically timeless realms of peace and harmony existing alongside the dusty and frustrating road of modern life ('The Other Side of the Hedge'), and he describes a strange Irish girl who personifies the spirit of the woods and turns into a tree by the end of her story ('Other Kingdom'). With these and other demonstrations of the relevance of Greek and Celtic myth to industrialised modern society, Forster sought to restore a forgotten reverence for the powers of nonhuman nature.

Welty's purposes in *The Wide Net* are somewhat different, for she wished to show how the forces embodied in myth are apparent both in recent history and in contemporary American life. She wished to affirm the existence of mysteries that most people simply ignore. Robert Penn Warren explained in the early 1940s, when the stories had just come out, that Welty operated within the main traditions of literary modernism when she developed this approach. Defending her practice against criticism that it was self-consciously allegorical, he wrote that she created

> a tissue of symbols which emerge from, and disappear into, a world of scene and action which, once we discount the author's special perspective, is recognizable in realistic terms. The method is similar to the method of much modern poetry, and to that of much modern fiction and drama (Proust, James, Kafka, Mann, Isak Dinesen, Katherine Anne Porter, Pirandello, Kaiser, Andreyev, O'Neill, for example); but at the same time it is a method as old as fable, myth, and parable.[7]

In particular, she used supernatural suggestions to emphasise the wonder of historical events like Aaron Burr's treason ('First Love') or meteorological events such as the equinox and their effect upon individual human consciousness ('The Winds'). Most importantly, fertility myth and its associated rituals provide the central symbolic emphasis for *The Wide Net*, representing the vital energy of four of the eight stories in the collection. Welty's long fascination with classical mythology and her response to Sir James Frazer's *Golden Bough* are fully apparent here for the first time.

'The Wide Net' is a comic, rural Mississippi version of fertility ritual which recalls the myth of the fisher-king and other motifs associated with baptismal plunges into deep sources of life. It recounts a daylong expedition to drag the Pearl River with a huge net to recover the drowned body of young William Wallace Jamieson's pregnant wife. This realistic event accumulates mythic associations as vast numbers of fish are dredged up and roasted for a Rabelaisian feast on the bank, and the King of the Snakes is sighted as a fortunate omen just before an enormous thunderstorm. Welty's descriptions bestow dimensions of the marvellous upon natural settings and actions that would otherwise seem less remarkable. Here, for instance, is the look of the approaching thunderstorm.

In the eastern sky were the familiar castles and the round towers to which they were used, gray, pink, and blue, growing darker and filling with thunder. Lightning flickered in the sun along their thick walls. But in the west the sun shone with such a violence that in an illumination like a long-prolonged glare of lightning the heavens looked black and white; all color left the world, the goldenness of everything was like a memory, and only heat, a kind of glamor and oppression, lay on their heads. The thick heavy trees on the other side of the river were brushed with mile-long streaks of silver, and a wind touched each man on the forehead. At the same time there was a long roll of thunder that began behind them, came up and down mountains and valleys of air, passed over their heads, and left them listening still. With a small, near noise a mockingbird followed it, the little white bars of its body flashing over the willow trees (*CS*, p. 182).

When the tired and sunburned procession of men and boys comes marching back into town after their heroic feat, they bring only strings of fish and one baby alligator. No sign has been seen of William Wallace's wife Hazel, whose suicide note set off the expedition to the river. She has been safe at home all day, having played this trick on her husband to punish him for staying out all night with his friends. Symbolically, she has forced him to undergo a trial and a ritual cleansing for betraying his bond to her. A rainbow curves over the roof of their house as the young husband returns, signifying the restoration of his happiness and a blessing on the marriage which his wife has caused him to reaffirm.

The three stories in *The Wide Net* of greatest interest from a feminist point of view are 'Asphodel', 'Livvie' and 'At the Landing'. They are all focused on the experience of women who encounter the masculine principle as it is embodied in a Dionysian figure. In each case, a carefully-ordered setting is disrupted by the entrance of the invigorating but also frightening male who carries a godlike energy about him. In every story the female characters are timid, passive creatures who are at the mercy of controlling men.

The supernatural associations of the invading male are most obvious in 'Asphodel', which recalls Forster's 'Story of a Panic' in its references to goats and the central action of Dionysian (or Pan-like) disruptions of a picnic. Welty's story is full of classical allusions, from its setting beside the Doric columns of a ruined plantation house, to proper names such as Sabina and Asphodel and Phoebe, and references to statues of Greek and Roman gods. A group of ageing maiden ladies is paying tribute to the town matriarch Miss Sabina the day after her funeral by picnicking by the ruins of Asphodel, the mansion of her disgraced and vanished husband. ('Miss Sabina' is called by her maiden name as was the traditional small-town custom in the South for 'ladies' whether or not they ever married.) A portent of coming events is provided by the comment of one of the ladies as they make their way across a little stream to the ruined house. ' "I used to be scared of little glades," said Phoebe. "I used to think something, something wild, would come and carry me off" ' (*CS*, p. 201).

Their picnic is dainty and sumptuous, all neatly spread out on a cloth, and when they have finished their repast, they press at the pomegranate stains on their mouths and begin to tell Miss Sabina's story to each other in serene voices. Any reader familiar with classical mythology would begin to grow uneasy at the mention of pomegranates, remembering that this fruit was sacred to Dionysos and that Persephone's eating even a few seeds created a bond between herself and her gloomy ravisher Pluton which even her powerful mother Demeter could not completely break. The devotees of Miss Sabina are clearly meant to be Sabines who are about to be ravished as they sit unsuspecting in their Mississippi glade.

The story they tell of Miss Sabina's disappointed life is centred on the depredations of her wild husband Mr Don McInnis. 'A great, profane man', he was the last of his line but full of procreative power. On his and Miss Sabina's wedding night, he looked dangerous, 'swaying with drink, trampling the scattered flowers', and his laughter was like a rage that pointed his eyebrows and changed his face. During his years with his wife, he flourished while she suffered and their children met tragic ends. 'He was unfaithful – maybe always – maybe once —' the ladies remind themselves, and finally his wife drove him out of the house with a whip (CS, pp. 202–203). As their story reaches its grotesque end with the death of the tyrannical witch that Miss Sabina became, there is a sudden shudder in the vines among the ruined columns of Mr Don's house, and a bearded man 'as rude and golden as a lion' steps out, completely naked. The maiden ladies flee screaming in chorus and climb back into their buggy. As they retreat from the scene, they are pursued by a herd of goats that leap out from behind the columns of Asphodel. Mr Don McInnis has appeared like the great god Pan and taken his revenge on his wife's timid followers, at least one of whom will cherish the intoxicating moment of danger for the rest of her life.

Mr Don McInnis and the masculine energy he represents
are ambiguous in this story. Ruth Vande Kieft sees him as
the representative of 'surging, irresistible, pagan joy', in
opposition to the extreme of order and control embodied
in Miss Sabina.[8] Attention to issues of gender and the
social context of Southern life, however, suggest that he
is a comic portrait of something darker – the violent,
drunken, irresponsible Southern gentleman who brings
ruin upon his family. Yet his power is breathtaking and
his appearance to the ladies almost godlike. Welty wants
to invest this figure with the dangerous but also energising
forces of life associated with the Greek god Dionysos and
satyrs like Pan who are his lesser embodiments. One thinks
of the way Aeschylus used his *Bacchae* to dramatise the
contradictory qualities of the great god capable of both
peaceful fertility and terrifying chaos. 'Asphodel' seems
ultimately to condemn Mr Don McInnis, in spite of his
frightening appeal. He dwells naked in the rubble of
his dynastic home, representing perhaps the end of the
Southern patriarchy that had erected a society which it
destroyed with its own excesses. Miss Sabina represents
a female realm which is forced by this patriarchy into a
ridiculous extreme of opposition. In the face of chaotic
violence, she erects an hysterical system of order which
also destroys itself.

'Livvie' presents a more benign incarnation of the male
fertility figure. The story is set in a black farming community and concerns a maiden in distress who is rescued
from imprisonment by a princely young man simply vi-
brating with colour and the forces of spring. Livvie has
married an old man who is rich by the standards of his
community. He owns his land and has field-hands working
it, but he is a typical miser who hoards his young wife as
he does all his other possessions. Welty is here reworking
folk materials familiar in the December/May marriages of
medieval tales such as Chaucer's 'The Merchant's Tale'.

She explicitly associates the old black man with winter.
Old Solomon has asked his 16-year-old bride before he
married her, 'if she was choosing winter, would she pine
for spring' (*CS*, p. 228). Livvie is too obedient and shy to
answer anything but no.

During the nine years of their marriage, however, she
has begun to yearn for something beyond the oppressive
quiet of her life with Solomon. By the time the story
opens, he is bedridden and sleeping most of the time. It
is springtime, and one day the forces of the new season
begin to invade their little house. 'The whole day, and the
whole night before, she had felt the stir of spring close to
her. It was as present in the house as a young man would
be' (*CS*, p. 231). Later in the day she goes on the first walk
she has ever dared to take beyond the protective bounds of
her husband's property, and on the Old Natchez Trace she
sees exactly such a young man. He wears pointed shoes,
peg-top pants, and bright socks.

> His coat long and wide and leaf-green he opened like
> doors to see his high-up tawny pants and his pants he
> smoothed downward from the points of his collar, and
> he wore a luminous baby-pink satin shirt. At the end,
> he reached gently above his wide platter-shaped round
> hat, the color of a plum, and one finger touched at the
> feather, emerald green, blowing up in the spring winds
> (*CS*, p. 235).

This vision of outrageous spring charm is both beautiful
and dangerous, however. He moves along, 'kicking the
flowers as if he could break through everything in the
way and destroy anything in the world'. Yet this destructive
power is exactly what is needed to break through the torpor
of winter and through the walls of isolation that old Solomon
has erected around his carefully-ordered house. Livvie feels
a chill when she witnesses the young man's 'abandon and

menace', but it excites her. She suspects that this young man, whose name is Cash, has already invaded Solomon's preserve by stealing enough money to buy the finery he wears.

Cash follows Livvie as she flees back into her house, and when he enters the bedroom of old Solomon behind her, 'there was a noise like a hoof pawing the floor'. The goat-god has appeared again. Solomon wakes for the last time, to see his young successor standing beside his wife, and he pronounces a kind of blessing upon them which is also an apology.

'So here come the young man Livvie wait for. Was no prevention. No prevention . . . .'

'God forgive Solomon for sins great and small. God forgive Solomon for carrying away too young girl for wife and keeping her away from her people and from all the young people would clamor for her back' (CS, p. 239).

He lifts up his hand and gives Livvie his most prized possession, his silver watch. Then he dies, and Livvie is embraced by Cash and whirled around in circles in the carefully-ordered sitting-room. The silver watch, with which Solomon had sought to order the passage of time, drops to the floor during this celebratory ritual. Livvie leaves the house with Cash, stepping out into 'the bursting light of spring'.

'At the Landing' is the most troubling of these three stories about the effects of masculine sexuality upon shy and vulnerable women. It begins as an upper-class white version of the same basic situation as that in 'Livvie': the incarceration of a young woman by an old man. In 'At the Landing' the maiden is Jenny Lockhart, whose grandfather has kept her carefully immured in the museum-like quiet of

his ancestral house in order to protect her from mysterious
forces which had destroyed her mother. The old man and
his granddaughter take their meals in a gazebo which Welty
describes as sitting on a knoll where a little breeze blows
from the Mississippi River three miles away. 'All about the
pavilion was an ancient circling thorny rose, like the initial
letter in a poetry book' CS, p. 242). Such a description
hints at fairytale analogues like the Grimm brothers' story
of Briar Rose, perhaps better known as Sleeping Beauty,
the princess enchanted in one hundred years' sleep behind
a barrier of thorns. From the enchanted stronghold of the
pavilion, Jenny and her grandfather often see the distant
figure of Billy Floyd, a wild young man who earns his
living by catching enormous fish in the Mississippi. He is
both the prince who will awaken her, and the destructive
force from which her grandfather seeks to protect her.

Like Livvie, Jenny is obedient to her keeper, and indeed
to anybody whom she encounters. At the same time, however, other potentials are suggested by her demeanour.

She was calm the way a child is calm, with never the
calmness of a spirit. But like a distant lightning that
silently bathes a whole shimmering sky, one awareness
was always trembling about her: one day she would be
free to come and go (CS, p. 242).

Her grandfather is near death as the story opens,
and he foresees the overthrow of his power, just as old
Solomon did on his deathbed in 'Livvie'. The grandfather
thinks of the forces of disorder as a flood of the Mississippi,
and his last words predict its coming. He has dreamed that
the mysterious and disreputable Billy Floyd has come and
warned him.

'The river has come back. That Floyd came to tell me.
The sun was shining full on the face of the church, and

that Floyd came around it with his wrist hung with a
great long catfish. . . .Oh, it came then! Like a horse.
A mane of cedar trees tossing over the top.'

. . . 'That Floyd's catfish has gone loose and free,' he
said gently, as if breaking news to someone. 'And all
of a sudden, my dear – my dears, it took its life back,
and shining so brightly swam through the belfry of the
church, and downstream' (CS, p. 240).

This description of Floyd is obviously phallic, with its
references to the church belfry, the powerful horse and
the 'great long catfish', a fish which also served as a fertility
symbol in 'The Wide Net'. The powerful, fertilising river is
Billy Floyd's element, and he comes and goes upon it as
mysteriously as its own currents flow.

Floyd is the Dionysian figure who will free Miss
Jenny from the lifelessness of her static world, as Welty
makes clear in the description of Jenny's first encounters
with the wild young man. Jenny is allowed to visit her
mother's grave in a little shady cemetery across a stream
from a sunny, wild-smelling pasture where Floyd first
appears close enough for her to see him distinctly. She
watches from the graveyard realm of the dead as Floyd
faces her in the sun, and then makes a phallic leap into
the ravine between them, smiles up at her and takes a long
drink from the spring in cupped hands. Another day he
performs another ritual which similarly prefigures sexual
union between himself and Jenny; as she watches from the
graveyard, he leaps upon the back of a red horse and races
around the pasture three times before moving up into the
woods.

Jenny is fascinated and frightened: 'she knew that he
lived apart in delight. That could make a strange glow fall
over the field where he was, and the world go black for her,
left behind. She felt terrified, as if at a pitiless thing' (CS,

p. 245). Yet she begins to love him and to understand that 'the secrecy of life was in the terror of it' (*CS*, p. 245). Her longing for him takes the image of a well, and she yearns to go to the bottom of the dark passage.

When her grandfather's dream comes to pass and the Mississippi rises in flood, Floyd takes Jenny in his boat to the high hill of the cemetery and consummates their strange courtship. Welty's description of the act explicitly connects it with the feminine sexual imagery of the well in Jenny's longings, but she also associates it with violence and death.

> When her eyes were open and clear upon him, he *violated* her and still he was without care or demand and as gay as if he were still clanging the bucket at the well. With the same thoughtlessness of motion, that was a kind of grace, he next *speared* a side of wild meat from an animal he had killed and had ready in his boat, and cooked it over a fire he had burning on the ground. (*CS*, p. 251). [my emphasis]

Billy Floyd violates Jenny Lockhart as cheerfully and thoughtlessly as he spears the piece of meat from the wild animal he has killed. These seem natural actions to be taken for granted, but as ensuing events demonstrate, the rape will have as terrible an effect on Miss Jenny as Floyd's assault had on the animal he now prepares to eat. Robert Penn Warren commented long ago on the strange conjunction of lighthearted language and terrible events in Welty's fiction, [9] and here we encounter its effect in especially troubling form.

The story ends with Miss Jenny having left her grandfather's house in search of Floyd and having arrived at a rough camp along the river to wait for him. The fishermen, who have been amusing themselves by throwing knives at a tree and who smell like the trees 'that had bled to the knives

they wore', turn their attention to their shy visitor. They put
her inside a grounded houseboat and rape her, one by one.
Welty's narrative tone here is strangely light and cheerful
for such a subject.

> When she called out, she did not call any name; it was a
> cry with a rising sound, as if she said 'Go back,' or asked
> a question, and then at the last protested. A rude laugh
> covered her cry, and somehow both the harsh human
> sounds could easily have been heard as rejoicing, going
> out over the river in the dark night. By the fire, little boys
> were slapped by their mothers – as if they knew that the
> original smile now crossed Jenny's face, and hung there
> no matter what was done to her, like a bit of color that
> kindles in the sky after the light has gone (*CS*, p. 258).

What is this 'original smile'? What does it mean?
Are we to assume that Eudora Welty celebrates gang
rape? She has left the conclusion of 'At the Landing'
deliberately ambiguous. On one hand the story suggests that
the forces of life are as destructive as vast floods and rape,
but that they also cause rejoicing. Yet the tenderness and
vulnerability of Jenny Lockhart make us wonder whether
the cost of her awakening can be borne. Her smile is like
the last bit of colour in a dying sky, and we cannot help
fearing that the life has left Jenny as the light has left the
sky in the analogy.

The final line of the story describes the young boys
in the encampment as they practise the arts of manhood,
here 'throwing knives with a dull *pit* at the tree'. It is hard
to imagine how a woman reader could think of that sound
as pleasant.

4 Demeter and Kore in Mississippi

'I'm a short-story writer who writes novels the hard way, and by accident,' Eudora Welty has said (*CNVRS*, p. 86). Her first true novel – and her masterpiece – began with a short story called 'The Delta Cousins' and then grew unexpectedly. She had produced *The Robber Bridegroom* under pressure from editors who felt that the legitimate form of important fiction was the novel, but that book is more a playfully extended tale than a novel. 'The Delta Cousins' was a story continuing the exploration of feminine encounters with masculine sexuality which was such an important element in *The Wide Net*. As Michael Kreyling has shown, the story presents 'the theme of innocence in the character of motherless, sensitive, nine-year-old Laura Kimball, shadowed but never touched by the world of "real" experience that threatens the peace and wonder of her private world'.[1] The sinister world of experience which Laura encounters is more particularly the world of adult sexuality represented by an old beekeeper who exposes himself in front of Laura and her cousin India. When she sent 'The Delta Cousins' to her agent Diarmuid Russell, he wrote back and said, 'Eudora, this is chapter two of a novel. Go on with it' (*CNVRS*, p. 180).

Neither Russell nor Welty herself could have predicted how the novel would shape itself, and indeed it took an entirely different course than the short story might have suggested. The time was the early 1940s, and wartime anxieties preoccupied most of the world. Welty's brothers

85

Edward and Walter were both on far-distant battlefronts, as were many of her friends. The horrors and destruction of war must have influenced her in defining a vision of human experience which could serve as an alternative. She says she cannot remember any planned structure but just wrote the pieeces as they occurred to her and sent them off to her friend John Robinson in Italy, to amuse him and remind him of home.[2] The narrative gradually defined its own form as a pastoral hymn of fertility and peace which owes much to the possibilities suggested by Virginia Woolf's dramatisation of family life centred on a mother's creative power in *To the Lighthouse*.

The significance of *Delta Wedding* can be appreciated most fully when Welty's novel is seen in a dialogic relationship to the masculine epic tradition of warfare, a polar relationship in which each form challenges the other as an ideal model of behaviour. Welty never pretended that the world of her novel was typical. She deliberately chose to set the novel in 1923.

> I had to pick a year – and this was quite hard to do – in which all the men could be home and uninvolved. It couldn't be a war year. It couldn't be a year when there was a flood in the Delta. . . . It had to be a year that would leave my characters all free to have a family story. . . . I wanted to write a story that showed the solidity of this family and the life that went on on a small scale in a world of its own.

She knew how atypical such periods of peace and stability are in human affairs, feeling that we live 'in a very precarious world without knowing it, always'. She took pains to make it implicit in the novel that the situation it pictured was 'a fragile, temporary thing' (*CNVRS*, pp. 49–50). *Delta Wedding* urges its readers to accept a constructive, life-giving feminine ideal as an alternative to the destructive, life-destroying masculine ideal of warfare that has figured so prominently in literary tradition since Homer's *Iliad*.

Welty alludes to the masculine arena of war within *Delta Wedding*, as a way of countering its cultural justifications. The First World War has destroyed one branch of the Fairchild family, by causing the death of heroic young Denis and the breakup of his small family. His widow is a wild-haired, perhaps deranged social outcast in the town, and their daughter, mentally retarded Maureen, who is sometimes maliciously destructive and sometimes manic, can be seen as a symbol of chaos.

Denis's brother George has taken his place as the family hero, but he too has been damaged by the war and needs his wife's support to make him whole. A major motivation of the novel's plot is the need to reunite the temporarily estranged Robbie with George to restore the potential for fertility and renewal in the family. George and Robbie's marriage is the model for Dabney's union with Troy Flavin which gives *Delta Wedding* its title. During Dabney's wedding near the end of the novel, Robbie basks in the warmth of her reunion with her husband, and muses about his blind need for her. She thinks back to 'the time where she had first held out her arms, back when he came in the store, home from the war, a lonely man that noticed wildflowers. She could not see why he needed to be so desperate! She loved him' (*DW*, p. 213).

The visual motif chosen by Dabney for her wedding derives from pastoral conventions that have come down to us from the Renaissance. The bridesmaids carry shepherds' crooks bedecked with flowers, and guests eat pastries shaped like cornucopias. John Edward Hardy was the first to notice these signs of *Delta Wedding*'s relation to the affirmative comic mode of Renaissance pastoral, with 'its wit, its merging of realism and magic, its delicacy, its formal and elegiac ironies, its universal mythiness'.[3] In the Renaissance pastoral, classical fertility myth represents the renewing and cleansing powers of the natural world. Shakespeare's romantic comedies employ the characteristically comic tone and movement toward consummation of young love in the celebration of wedding. *A Midsummer Night's Dream*, *As You Like It* and *The Tempest* all present the characteristic pastoral flight from corrupt court to enchanted natural retreat. There lovers endure confusion as an initiation but are finally united in triumphant ritual. Despite pastoral transformations, however, sojourners in the timeless world of ritual renewal must return to civilisation to take up their lives in mundane reality, where time, pain and death hold sway.

Whatever Welty's conscious awareness of Renaissance pastoralism may have been, these same patterns are at work in the charmed and protected world of Shellmound. Hardy points out that as a backdrop to family life in the plantation house during the wedding preparations, a friend of the bride plays interminably on the piano in a way which transforms the house and its occupants into a forest realm. At a particular moment of crisis, when George Fairchild's estranged wife suddenly appears, Mary Lamar begins to play, and 'like the dropping of rain or the calling of a bird the notes came from another room, effortless and endless, isolated from them, yet near, and sweet like the guessed existence of mystery. It made the house like a nameless forest, wherein many little lives lived privately, each to its lyric pursuit and its shy protection' (*DW*, p. 156).

The experience of reading the novel performs a similar transformation for its readers because it places some of the most painful problems of domestic life in a setting which affirms the possibility of affection, cooperation, and renewal. *Delta Wedding* is a timeless garden centred on the cycles of nature and the feminine which Ellen Fairchild embodies as mother of the family. Welty emphasises the close links between the natural world and feminine experience in a description of Ellen's thoughts as she rides in a wagon with her husband near the end of the novel. 'The repeating fields, the repeating cycles of season and her own life – there was something in the monotony itself that was beautiful, rewarding – perhaps to what was womanly within her. . . . They rolled on and on. It was endless. The wheels rolled, but nothing changed' (*DW*, p. 240).

As readers we experience the pastoral sojourn by entering the Delta with nine-year-old Laura McRaven, who is chiefly conscious of her age and the loss of her mother. Like Laura, we also bear a burdensome awareness of time and death, but through participation in the feminine rituals of hearth, meadow, wood, labyrinth, beehive and sacred river, we will be initiated into the eternal cycles of fertility. At the end of the novel, we return to the world of time as Laura herself decides to do. And even the plantation domain of Shellmound is preparing for change.

Such a version of pastoral is very different from the dominant masculine traditions of pastoral escape in American literature. From Cooper's Deerslayer novels, Melville's sea stories and Twain's *Huckleberry Finn* to more recent versions of the pattern like Faulkner's *The Bear* and Bellow's *Henderson the Rain King*, American heroes have been seeking to recover a kind of prelapsarian innocence by fleeing into nature to evade the corruption and complexity which they associate with civilisation and the feminine.[4] This pattern has served to mask or rewrite a history of masculine guilt for the consequences of westward migration – the slaughter of red Indians and vastly destructive exploitation of natural resources in the American landscape.[5] William Faulkner's epics of Mississippi life communicate an anguished understanding of this problem, but he can provide no hope for its resolution. In contrast, the pastoral vision of *Delta Wedding* depicts a community of women and men cooperating with each other in harmony with the landscape. Thus Shellmound plantation stands as an answer to Faulkner's tragic and decaying Mississippi patriarchies by emphasising the maternal centre of family life which supports cooperation and revitalisation.

Virginia Woolf's *To the Lighthouse* helped Welty understand how to develop the ideas of distinctly feminine fertility and community which existed merely as germs in 'The Delta Cousins'. Intertextual links between Woolf's novel and *Delta Wedding* suggest how Welty answered and extended the themes of marriage and the unifying role of the mother which Woolf established as important literary themes in her depiction of the Ramsay family. Welty seems to be unconsciously agreeing with Woolf's implied argument for the central power of womanhood.

In transforming 'The Delta Cousins' from a short story about a nine-year-old girl's uneasy encounter with masculine sexuality into a hymn of feminine fertility, Welty created a mother figure equal in sensitivity to Woolf's Mrs Ramsay and similarly employed multiple points of view on focal characters and events. As in *To the Lighthouse*, Welty renders the swirl of family life in flashes, glimpses, fleeting moments, often in the life of children, for whose portrayal she has a special gift. Like Mrs Ramsay, Ellen Fairchild is the central figure unifying the family, notably in resolving a crisis precipitated by her sister-in-law Robbie's angry challenge to family solidarity. Most important in *Delta Wedding*, however, is the dramatisation of the wider network of family life around the central event of the wedding. Welty's novel unfolds almost entirely through feminine perspectives. These seem to take their form naturally and unconsciously from the oldest wedding story our culture has preserved with a feminine perspective – the myth of Demeter and Kore, archetypal mother and daughter. Point of view in the novel alternates between Ellen Fairchild and her many daughters, both natural and surrogate. The story begins with nine-year-old Laura McRaven's experience in journeying from her city home in Jackson to the plantation of her Fairchild cousins, where she will become a surrogate daughter to her Aunt Ellen and seek acceptance in the family. The perspective then shifts to Ellen as she comforts her motherless niece and broods over the coming marriage of her daughter Dabney. The interaction between Ellen and her various daughters continues to shift the novel's perspectives among women and girls as they reflect upon courtship, marriage and family – a progression dramatised in the ritual events leading to Dabney's wedding. The end of the novel rounds out the opening symmetry, with Laura's final vision.

Where men and women gazed and marvelled at Mrs Ramsay in *To the Lighthouse*, the women of *Delta Wedding* focus their adoring attention on a man, George Fairchild, who Ellen realises has inherited his dead brother Denis's function as both hero and sacrificial beast for the whole family (*DW*, p. 63). Two relative outsiders to the main family unit at Shellmound corroborate Ellen's musings, but in a spirit of defence, wishing to protect him from the pressure of such extravagant demands. Storing up love for her Uncle George, Laura wishes Shellmound would burn down so that she could rescue him (*DW*, p. 76). George's estranged wife Robbie also fiercely strives to protect him, feeling that she is the only person who 'could hold him against that grasp, that separating thrust of Fairchild love' and that he is lost without her (*DW*, pp. 148–9).

By making George the epitome of family virtues, the vitaliser and protector upon whom they all depend, his family deny him subjectivity. A hero cannot afford human vulnerabilities but instead must exist only for the needs of others. In the terms of cinematic criticism, the Fairchild family gaze upon George is thus basically exploitative. Viewed from outside by his demanding relatives, he is heroic, but within himself he is a mere mortal wounded by the horrors he encountered in the war, outside the pastoral haven of Shellmound. He must be sustained by women who understand him as a vulnerable person – who see him with a gaze of mutuality and sympathy – as Ellen and Laura do from a distance and Robbie does intimately and essentially as his wife.

Ultimately George's dependence on Robbie and his relation to everyone else in the family are positive, cooperative and complementary. Unlike Woolf's Mr Ramsay, who exhaustingly demands sympathy from women to prop up his confidence so that he can maintain his lonely heroic outpost of intellectual struggle, George gives as much as he takes. He never intrudes upon the integrity of others, but only intervenes occasionally to prevent genuine danger. Dabney understands this as she watches her uncle allow a butterfly to flutter by his face without moving to frighten it, but her mother knows more fully his respect for the world outside him. 'Only George left the world she knew as pure – in spite of his fierce energies, even heresies, as he found it; still real, still bad, still fleeting and mysterious and hopelessly alluring to her' (DW, p. 80). Woolf deconstructed the traditional male concept of heroic self-sufficiency in her ironic portrait of Mr Ramsay. Welty continues the process, providing a feminine redefinition of male heroism which grants its operative powers but denies its pretensions to self-sufficiency and its demands for domination.

Delta Wedding shares with To the Lighthouse an appropriate setting for the celebration of fertility in the context of family life. Both novels take place in September under a harvest moon, in a family sanctuary removed from the disruptions and demands of public life. Woolf's scene is the house in the Isle of Skye where the Ramsay family customarily spend their late summer holiday, and most of the novel celebrates the festive atmosphere created by Mrs Ramsay. As we have seen, Welty placed her novel in a time in Mississippi history when no natural or human catastrophes could intrude upon the domestic community she wanted to explore. Both Mrs Ramsay and

Ellen Fairchild preside over a garden paradise where the youngest of their eight children frolic and the older ones learn about courtship and marriage which their mothers are promoting or supporting. Mrs Ramsay subtly manipulates Paul Rayley's proposal to Minta Doyle and plans to lead other 'victims' to the marriage altar while her nubile daughter Prue basks wonderingly in the glow surrounding Paul and Minta. Ellen Fairchild directs the preparations for Dabney's wedding, strives to sympathise with the unwelcome bridegroom, and provides necessary mediation in reconciling George and Robbie.

Welty's novel differs sharply from Woolf's in its essentially comic outcome. While *To the Lighthouse* begins in a celebratory mode and the long first section ends with the union of lovers expected in comedy, the novel grows much darker in the last two sections. Time, war, and disease creep into the summer home and into the Ramsay family in 'Time Passes', destroying most of Mrs Ramsay's accomplishments. She herself dies, her promising mathematician son Andrew is killed in the war, her daughter Prue dies of pregnancy complications a few months after a brilliant wedding, and the marriage of Paul Rayley and Minta Doyle quickly turns sour. The novel's final section, 'The Lighthouse', returns to the house ten years after Mrs Ramsay's death and presents a saddened group of fewer than half the number of the original boisterous congregation.

Shellmound plantation is surrounded by potential dangers and described with ironies which prevent the reader's complacent acceptance of appearances, but Welty's novel consistently affirms the possibility of fertility and community. The name and topography of the plantation imply its paradoxical significance. Shellmound is located in the heart of the rich Mississippi river delta whose shape recalls ancient motifs of female fertility and whose topsoil is so deep as to seem inexhaustible. The plantation takes its name from an Indian mound in one of the cotton

fields. Welty describes it through Dabney's eyes as she
looks at the place where she first noticed the mysterious
and slightly sinister overseer who would be her husband:
'And she looked with joy, as if it marked the preeminent
place, at the Indian mound topped with trees like a masted
green boat on the cottony sea' (*DW* pp. 30–31). This fertile
protuberance brings together the lovers whose wedding is
the novel's consummation, but the mound itself is the
remnant of a lost world. Thus it suggests the regenerative
power of ancient places and their relics.

Previous commentators have noticed that the shell reference in the mound's – and the plantation's – name suggest
a certain protected and empty quality in the social world
centred there, but Mississippi history reveals an ancient
potential for something very different in the landscape.
Welty's Shellmound may have been suggested by an actual
place, a tiny community not far from Greenwood that was
named for a nearby Indian mound with mussel shells on
its top. In a larger sense, Indian mounds like the one in
the novel are a distinctive part of the Delta landscape, left
behind by the Middle Mississippian Indian civilisation of
mound-builders who were culturally related to the Mayas
of Central America. The inheritors of those ancient monu-
ments, the Choctaws, call one of these mounds 'The Great
Mother' and regard it as the birthplace of their race. At the
centre of the mound, they say, the Great Spirit created the
first Choctaws, who crawled through a hole or cave into the
light of day.[6]

Eudora Welty knows about the Choctaw traditions
associated with the mounds and specifically about 'The
Great Mother'. She may have placed the fertile mound at
the centre of her fictional plantation in order to expand the
sense of power in the Delta landscape by associating it with
the primordial feminine forces of generation embodied in
the Choctaw legends. There is no doubt that she consciously
employed another such frame of symbolic reference in the

novel, that of a well-known myth with obvious fertility emphasis. Dabney's suitor Troy, first associated with the mound rising from the rich bottomland, is a threatening figure who on the social level is not considered a suitable husband and on a symbolic level is a rapacious intruder like the god of the underworld who ravished Demeter's daughter Kore, or Persephone. Welty says that such associations came to her when she first saw the Delta, and they are essential to the meaning of *Delta Wedding*.[7]

Combining associations of fertility with the general sense of the shellmound as a remnant of a past culture, Welty is able to make a complex point about the revitalisation of another outmoded way of life – the antebellum Southern tradition associated with Fairchild family legends. For all their charm, the family remain essentially childish because of their habit of retreating from trouble and mythologising their past to make it pretty and comforting. Robbie, a lower-class outsider like Troy, knows that the world the Fairchilds have fabulated is unreal. With a hardheaded desire born of poverty, she wants honesty that will allow her 'to touch the real, undeceiving world within the fairy Shellmound world to love George' (*DW*, p. 149). Because her marriage with George is reaffirmed, we know that she and Troy will ultimately revitalise the outmoded 'aristocratic' world of Shellmound plantation by their marriages into it.

Welty's interest in dramatising a maternally sustained family may have been stimulated by Woolf's, but it should be obvious in the above discussion of narrative techniques and setting that her mode of developing these approaches is entirely her own. She had in mind the particularly feminine quality of Delta plantation society as she described the life of the Fairchild family in her novel. 'In the Delta it's very much of a matriarchy,' she explains, 'especially in those years in the twenties that I was writing about, and really ever since the Civil War when the men were all gone and the women began to take over everything. You know, they really did. I've met families up there where the women just ruled the roost, and I've made that happen in the book because I thought, that's the way it was in those days in the South' (*CNVRS*, p. 304).

The Woolfian echoes that link *Delta Wedding* intertextually with *To the Lighthouse* thus alert us as much to Welty's distinctive creation of her own mother-centred fictional universe as they testify to Woolf's role in suggesting new subjects and modes of writing. In commenting on how she came upon Woolf's novel 'absolutely cold and it just knocked me out', Welty affirms that although she does not directly allude to Woolf in her work, 'the sense of what she has done certainly influenced me as an artist' (*CNVRS*, p. 325). If we examine a few more of the subtle but specific ways in which that influence links the two novels, we will see how Welty weaves suggestions from *To the Lighthouse* into her own development of the closely interrelated themes of motherhood and female sexuality. Both novels contain scenes of motherly care for children. *To the Lighthouse* opens with Mrs Ramsay measuring a stocking on her son's leg. 'Stand still. Don't be tiresome,' says Mrs Ramsay to James.[8] While this event provides a long and central scene for Woolf's novel, there is only a fleeting reference to such fitting of clothes in *Delta Wedding*. It comes in a very different kind of situation, but is similarly associated with the role of motherhood. Ellen Fairchild sees a mysterious girl in the bayou woods while she is looking for a lost piece of jewellery, and the encounter becomes a mystic conjunction of symbolic mother and daughter by the end of the scene. The revelation begins when Ellen commands the shy stranger to come out from her hiding place behind a tree; as the beautiful girl reveals herself, 'a whole mystery of life' opens up for Ellen.

'Stand still', said Ellen.
It was a thing she said habitually, often on her knees

with pins in her mouth. . . . She felt sometimes like a
mother to the world, all that was on her! yet she had
never felt a mother to a child this lovely (*DW*, p. 70).

Ellen Fairchild is shown putting children to bed, as Mrs
Ramsay does also, in the timeless maternal act of soothing
and reassuring children so that they feel safe enough to fall
asleep. For Woolf, this event is only a minor event after
the triumph of Mrs Ramsay's dinner party. For Welty,
however, Ellen's soothing Bluet to sleep emphasises the
themes of courtship and sexual initiation associated with
her lost garnet pin, at the same time that it pays tribute
to maternal comforting of children. Ellen tells her small
daughter the dream she has had about the pin her husband
had given her during courtship.

Mama dreamed about a thing she lost long time ago
before you were born. It was a little red breastpin,
and she wanted to find it. Mama put on her beautiful
gown and she went to see. She went to the woods by
James's Bayou, and on and on. She came to a great big
tree. . . . Hundreds of years old, never chopped down,
that great big tree. And under the tree was sure enough
that little breastpin (*DW*, pp. 64–5).

The dream is prophetic, for after Bluet has drifted into her
nap her mother goes out into the woods and encounters the
mysterious girl by such a tree. This Kore figure will prove
to have an important symbolic connection with the lost pin,
both representing the feminine and the loss traditionally
associated with sexual initiation. Welty's use of the motif
of a lost pin recalls Minta Doyle's lost brooch in *To the
Lighthouse*. In Woolf's novel the brooch is only mentioned
in passing as an heirloom Minta loses on the beach when
Paul Rayley proposes marriage to her. It represents both
female family tradition and Minta's virginity, jewels she

forfeits by her alliance with a man. As we shall see in the following pages, Welty's development of the motif is more complex.

One final symbol in Woolf that Welty uses to explore the theme of human fertility is bees. Bees are associated with Mrs Ramsay to imply her queenliness and the hivelike refuge she creates around herself. At one point Lily Briscoe imagines that she attracts people as a hive does, and that from a distance she has 'an august shape; the shape of a dome' (pp. 79–80). Later, in tribute to his wife's triumph at the dinner party, Mr Ramsay recites a poem which associates her with the fertile imagery of gardens and bees. 'Come out and climb the garden path, Luriana Lurilee./ The China rose is all abloom and buzzing with the yellow bee' (p. 166). Similar associations cluster about Welty's references to bees, as further discussion of *Delta Wedding* will demonstrate. When Welty uses these motifs, she weaves them as bright threads in a tapestry of ritual and myth celebrating the cycle of human fertility in harmony with the landscape.

The myths Welty uses to support this vision derive from some of our culture's deepest sources. It is easy to see why Welty was drawn to the story of Demeter because she and her daughter Persephone are the figures who naturally come to mind when one thinks of images of feminine power and relationship in classical mythology. Less widely known is Demeter's ancient connection with Dionysos, although a writer as late as Euripides testifies in his *Bacchae* that the two are the oldest deities. Sir James Frazer set them side by side in *The Golden Bough*, and we know how important that work was to Eudora Welty. It is impossible to know how consciously Welty worked out the relationship between Demeter and Dionysos, but careful reading of Frazer would have taught her about the widespread religious motif of mother goddess and male consort in early agricultural civilisations. In recent years archaeologists and mythographers have found evidence linking them to Neolithic religion and revealing corresponding functions and powers which Frazer implied and which Welty makes central to the pastoral world of *Delta Wedding*.

The Homeric Hymn to Demeter is the oldest written form of the Greek version of these ancient materials. It describes the abduction of Demeter's daughter the Kore (Persephone) from a flowery meadow by Hades (Pluton /Plutos), god of the underworld. Demeter's grief, the aid of her sister goddess Hecate of the underworld, the punishment of all creation for the rape by the Great Mother's withholding of fertility, then finally its restoration on the return of Persephone – these events define 'the most pervasive of all Greek Divine tales', according to mythographer G. S. Kirk. The most powerful rituals of Greek religion – the Eleusinian Mysteries – were established by Demeter in the Homeric Hymn to commemorate her grief and her daughter's return. Most scholars believe that the hymn serves to explain or justify a religious practice already in existence and of pre-Greek origins. Although the issue is still controversial, analysis of Mycenaean clay tablets in Linear-B dating back to the same period as the remains at Eleusis makes Dionysos's pre-Greek origins and close associations with Demeter increasingly certain.[9]

In the worship of Dionysos, as well as in the Homeric Hymns, meadowlike dancing grounds were sacred places where circle-dances promoted fertility and associated maidens with growing plants, as in the Homeric Hymn 'To Earth, the Mother of All'. The hymn sings of the great nourisher of all life and of her gift of 'fruitful land' – αρσυρα – a word often used metaphorically to denote woman as bearing seed and fruit. Those blessed by Mother Earth have children who are like the fruits of the soil. In particular, the hymn says that 'their daughters in flowerladen bands play and skip merrily over the soft flowers of the field'. This scene is much like the blissful meadow where Persephone and her maiden companions gathered flowers when Hades suddenly appeared.[10] These backgrounds are very important for an understanding of Eudora Welty's treatment of landscape and human fertility in *Delta Wedding*. In particular we must recognise the erotic feminine quality of the landscape in these traditions and remember its connection with the complementary deities Demeter and Dionysos, to see how Welty revives their symbolic force in the charmed maternal world of her novel.

As Laura McRaven enters the Delta at the beginning of the novel, the landscape is described as having a dreamy, fertile quality that completely overwhelms the rational mind.

Thoughts went out of her head and the landscape filled it. . . . The land was perfectly flat and level but it shimmered like the wing of a lighted dragonfly. It seemed strummed, as though it were an instrument and something had touched it. . . .

In the Delta the sunsets were the reddest light. The sun went down lopsided and wide as a rose on a stem in the west, and the west was a milk-white edge, like the foam of the sea. The sky, the field, the little track, and the bayou, over and over – all that had been bright or dark was now one color. From the warm window sill the endless fields glowed like a hearth in firelight. . . . (*DW*, pp. 4–5).

In *Literary Women* Ellen Moers points to this vision of the Delta as the one clearly female landscape in Eudora Welty's fiction, similar in a general sense to other open, sweeping terrains in women's writing which she finds to be places of self-assertion.[11] One of the most famous of these is the moors of *Jane Eyre*, where the heroine experiences a lonely independence under the guidance of a maternal deity. Kate Chopin's *The Awakening* presents the ocean and a Kentucky meadow as two other such settings, and Willa Cather's western plains and canyons function in a similar way for major characters in *My Antonia* and *The Song of the Lark*. Moers identifies such terrains with the contours of women's bodies and suggests that ravines and springs or rivers are particularly erotic landmarks. Such habits of mind are very old, for we have seen similarly feminine settings in the meadow where Persephone played with her girlish companions and the open pastures where Maenads worshipped their god Dionysos. The Greek materials not only dramatise the eroticism and fertility of woman and land, but also their vulnerability to masculine forces of violent disruption. Women writers of the modern period have also been aware of the dangers attendant upon feminine assertion, as we see in Jane Eyre's near-starvation on the moors, Edna Pontellier's drowning in *The Awakening*, and the seduction and abandonment of Cather's Antonia. But Ellen Moers alerts us to the distinctive uses women writers make of feminine topography. Brontë and Cather insist on the ultimately triumphant powers of woman and landscape, and while Chopin follows her indecisive heroine to defeat, the process serves to protest the repressive limits on women's lives by voicing the subjective experience of one woman who struggles to break free.

Eudora Welty presents her glowing, hearthlike Delta as a complex feminine topography embodying forces of both life and death. The landscape contains dark waters and is swept by violent changes of weather, just as its human inhabitants have inherited a bloody history and are threatened by racial violence which seethes under the graceful surface of plantation life. Ultimately, however, the land is fertile, and the matriarchal life of the Fairchild family prospers despite threats to its stability.

On the day before her wedding, Dabney takes an

early-morning ride on her new filly, and Welty uses
the occasion to depict her youthful feminine assertiveness
in harmony with the landscape. Her movement across the
dewy land prefigures her movement into full womanhood
which her marriage will bring. Dabney tiptoes out before
any of the family is awake, 'into the early eastern light which
already felt warm and lapping against her face and arms.'
The freshly-awakened land seems to welcome the girl and
her little horse.

> Flocks of birds flew from the fields, the little filly went
> delightedly through the wet paths, breasting and breaking
> the dewy nets of spider webs. Opening morning-glories
> were turned like eyes on her pretty feet. The occasional
> fences smelled sweet, their darkened wood swollen with
> night dew like sap, and following her progress the bayou
> rustled within, ticked and cried. The sky was softly blue
> all over, the last rim of sunrise cloud melting into it like
> the foam on fresh milk (*DW*, p. 120).

One is tempted to recall the fertile pastures of Euripides'
Bacchae, where the Maenads had only to touch the earth
to make milk and honey flow forth, for the scene is one of
complete peace and harmony between woman and fruitful
earth.

As she rides across the fields to visit the beautiful old
house where she and Troy will live after their marriage, she
inwardly rebels against the patriarchal Southern tradition of
'honor' and the bloody sacrifices it had exacted in duels and
Civil War defeat. 'I will never give up anything,' she vows.
This assertion of feminine practicality runs completely
counter, not only to the masculine code of honour, but
also to the self-sacrificing ideal of Southern womanhood
that her mother represents. A rejection of the physical
cowardice and sexual reticence of earlier generations of
Southern ladies is implied by her behaviour on her way

back home. She dares to look at the 'creepy and scary' whirlpool in the thick bayou woods, scene of family legends about ghosts and drownings. Here once in childhood, she had seen her wild young uncles Denis and George emerge naked from swimming and interrupt a knife-fight between two black boys. But on this day before her wedding, Dabney gazes into the whirlpool in a vertigo of sexual fascination. The whirlpool is an erotic feminine place into which she takes her last look as a virgin.

She parted the thonged vines of the wild grapes, *thick as legs*, and looked in. There it was. She gazed feasting her fear on the dark, vaguely stirring water.

There were more eyes than hers – frog eyes – snake eyes? She listened to the silence and then heard it stir, churn, churning in the early morning. She saw how the snakes were turning and moving in the water, passing across each other just below the surface, and now and then a head horridly sticking up. The vines and the cypress roots twisted and grew together on the shore and in the water more thickly than any roots should grow, gray and red, and some roots too *moved and floated like hair* (DW, p. 123). [my emphasis]

The connection between water and sexuality is reinforced by Welty's description of Dabney after her honeymoon, laughing with her husband at a family picnic. 'In catching sight of love she had seen both banks of a river and the river rushing between – she saw everything but the way down. Even now, lying in Troy's bared arm like a drowned girl, she was timid of the element itself' (DW, p. 245). The Yazoo River has similar symbolic associations for nine-year-old Laura.

Welty links this wide plantation vista of cottonfields and bayous to the myth of Demeter by allusions to Troy Flavin's frightening godlike qualities and by attributing to Ellen

Fairchild a fear that comes straight out of the myth. In the scene where Dabney, her nine-year-old sister India and her cousin Laura encounter Troy as they ride horseback across the Mound Field, Dabney thinks back to first noticing him there a year before, as she now watches his distant figure riding across her path on his black horse, his arm raised in greeting like a gun against the sky. She shuts her eyes and sees 'a blinding light, or else it was a dark cloud – that intensity under her flickering lids. . . . She thought of him proudly (he was right back of the mound now, she knew), a dark thundercloud, his slowness rumbling and his laugh flickering through in bright flashes' (*DW*, pp. 31–2). At the end of the novel, Troy still seems to have lightning playing about him (*DW*, p. 242). Welty knew that storm and earthquake, attributes of Zeus and Poseidon, could be associated with their brother Hades. Indeed, Hades was often called Zeus.

If Troy Flavin's positive qualities can be stimulated, he, like Hades/Pluton, will become a source of new riches from the feminine earth. When Persephone returned from her underworld marriage, her mother welcomed her like a Maenad and the land burst forth in fruit. Something similar is possible with Troy, as Welty suggests when she describes his arrival at the plantation house with a womblike sack full of his mother's quilts which symbolise both the traditional feminine art of the mountain people from whom Troy descends and the fertility of the landscape which he and Dabney will imitate. As Troy displays the quilts, he declares his choice of the one called Delectable Mountains to cover the marriage bed; 'that's the one I aim for Dabney and me to sleep under most generally, warm *and* pretty.' The sexual connotations of the bedroom landscape are not lost on Dabney's aunts, especially when Troy says she should wait to thank his mother until she has tried the quilts. 'That's what will count with Mammy. She might come if we have a baby, sure enough' (*DW*, p. 113).

Before Troy's hopes can be realised, however, the
bride must be blessed by the keepers of matriarchal family
traditions, and threats to the wedding must be removed by
epithalamion rituals including a symbolic trip to the underworld which echoes the Eleusinian Mysteries. In order to
trace the passage of these rituals, we must be familiar with
the other major actors in the rites and their symbolic presence in *Delta Wedding*.

We have seen how Welty associates Troy with the
Hades or Pluton of the Persephone myth. While everyone
knows his important role, few are aware of his connections
with Dionysos. In fact, the abduction of Persephone in the
Homeric Hymn occurs on the Nysan Plain, named after
the sacred mountain of Dionysos's birth and perhaps even
echoed in the second syllable of his name.[12] If he is the
god of the place where Persephone is kidnapped, then he
is closer to Hades than we are accustomed to thinking. In
Delta Wedding, a character with attributes of Dionysos is a
kind of double for Troy.

As John Allen has shown, the name Denis is a contraction
of 'Dionysos', and Denis Fairchild has mythic qualities that
are shared by his brother George.[13] Adoring women in the
family refer to Denis's wildness and his Maenad wife and
daughter, and even though he is dead, he remains the
epitome of family honour. His sister Tempe thinks, 'Denis
was the one that looked like a Greek God, Denis who
squandered away his life loving people too much, was too
kind to his family, was torn to pieces by other people's
misfortune, married beneath him, threw himself away in
drink, got himself killed in the war'. Tempe identifies
Denis's excessive energies with the haunts of the wood-
god Pan, who is of course simply another manifestation of
Dionysos. 'These fields and woods are still full of Denis,
full of Denis,' she says; 'If I were to set foot out there
by myself, . . . I'd meet the spirit of Denis Fairchild first
thing.' Dabney responds to this comment about her dead

uncle by looking over at his daughter Maureen, who, 'eyeing her, stuck out her tongue through her smiling and fruit-filled mouth' (*DW*, pp. 116–17). Such a description is plausible on a realistic level, but it also clearly links Maureen to the fertile Bacchic abandon associated with her father.

After his death, Denis's function has been assumed by George, similarly adored by all the women in the family as both saviour and sacrificial beast. In a moment of typically reckless bravery two weeks before the action of the novel begins, he has performed the part of St George by defeating a 'dragon' which threatened to kill Denis's daughter. That dragon is also the intruding urban machine in the pastoral garden – the train which brings Laura from the city to attend the wedding but also kills the mysterious nymph Ellen met in the bayou woods, as it nearly killed George and Maureen on the trestle. George's heroic near self-sacrifice is ultimately secondary to the underlying Dionysian qualities which Allen has shown to define his almost magical charm. These are apparent at the climax of the novel, when George arrives at Shellmound to find that Robbie has come back to him, and he stands with shoulders bare 'as a Greek God's, his hair on his forehead, as if he were intoxicated, unconscious of the leaf caught there, looking joyous' (*DW*, p. 166).

On a symbolic level George is the appropriate consort for the central Demeter figure of Ellen Fairchild. Although the mythic associations in the novel can be confusing, it is necessary only to keep in mind the Protean nature of these ancient traditions and to understand that they serve merely as suggestive references to intensify meaning. To understand the way these work themselves out in the overall movement of *Delta Wedding*, ordinary events must be seen to carry a mythic aura. In this mythic dimension Ellen represents a Demeter who has many daughters (some who are only daughter-surrogates, such as her nieces Laura and Maureen, her sister-in-law Robbie, and the mysterious nymph she meets in the woods) and whose proper symbolic consort is George. As Michael Kreyling demonstrates, there are many important moments of sympathetic harmony between Ellen and George, without any suggestion of disloyalty to their mates.[14] At these moments, Ellen and George function as presiding spirits over the family wedding preparations, representing the benign fertility of female and male.

In realistic matrimonial terms, however, George is closely associated with Troy Flavin. His marriage to Robbie is a kind of mirror image of Troy and Dabney's, with each Fairchild choosing a socially 'unworthy' mate, just as Denis had 'married beneath' himself. George's separation from his wife therefore suggests that such marriages do not work and threatens Dabney's chance of happiness with Troy. A quarrel over George's foolhardy attempt to save Maureen from the train has brought their marriage close to disaster. As promoter of wedding fertility, Ellen must somehow arrange their reconciliation if Dabney's wedding is to be propitious. A series of preparatory rituals leads up to the climactic confrontation between Ellen and Robbie, who has returned to find her husband but is full of bitterness toward the self-satisfied Fairchild clan. Ellen faces Robbie's anger and restores her to George, thus removing the threat to Dabney's marriage and, in a larger sense, the danger to family harmony. Then all that remains is a blessing of the bride and groom's house and an initiation to prepare Laura as a flower girl so that the wedding can proceed auspiciously.

The first ephitalamion ritual comes in effect at the hearth, the evening of Laura's arrival at Shellmound at the beginning of the novel. Ellen takes her niece into the big plantation kitchen to help her bake a coconut cake whose recipe is a feminine family secret. In this passage Welty puts into practice her view that food is a kind of language and describes a scene close to her memory of helping her own mother make cakes in her childhood.[15] In this sophisticated semiotic performance, Welty anticipates such

decoding of popular culture as Roland Barthes' *Mythologies*.
While she works the ingredients together, Ellen worries
about Dabney's happiness, but the act of combining sugar,
butter, eggs and flour in the proper order becomes a kind of
sympathetic magic as she associates the cake with a memory
of George and Robbie's amorous play in the Yazoo River at
a family picnic, when George carried his almost naked and
dripping wife up from the river and then lay smiling with
her on a bed of vines and flowers in the moonlight. The
cake will be an embodiment of the happiness George and
Robbie symbolise as precursors for Dabney and Troy, but
Ellen cannot be certain the recipe will work.

> As Ellen put in the nutmeg and the grated lemon rind
> she diligently assumed George's happiness, seeing it in
> the Fairchild aspects of exuberance and satiety; if it was
> unabashed, it was the best part true. But – adding the
> milk, the egg whites, the flour, carefully and alternately
> as Mashula's recipe said – she could be diligent and still
> not wholly sure – never wholly (*DW*, p. 26).

Later in the novel, a complementary magic cake will
be needed to fulfil Ellen's hopes. That cake will be a
black aphrodisiac patticake made by the Negro matriarch
Partheny, and it will be tasted by Troy, Robbie, and the
servant girl Pinchy who is 'coming through' puberty to
womanhood.

Dabney's visit to her maiden aunts Jim Allen and
Primrose at the Grove, the original plantation house
down on the Yazoo River, is the next important ritual
in the novel. Peggy Prenshaw has explained how these
aunts serve as virginal priestesses of family tradition,
passing down stories of matriarch Mary Shannon Fairchild
to the children of the family and preserving feminine arts of
cooking and sewing. They guard the sacred texts – Mashula
Hines's cookbook and Mary Shannon's diary 'full of things

to make and the ways to set out cuttings and the proper times, along with all her troubles and provocations' as a pioneer wife in the tangled Mississippi wilderness of one hundred years past. As Dabney leaves to return home, the aunts insist that she accept a precious heirloom from this immaculate museum as a wedding present: the little china night light that has comforted generations of Fairchilds in the dark. The little lamp holds mystery and family tradition which Welty associates in one of her essays with fiction itself.[16] In *Delta Wedding* this fiction is the family legends that tell of the heroic taming of the wilderness and *include* the central participation of the women in the family, unlike conventional textbook histories that credit the achievement solely to males. The Fairchild family legends also include in microcosm the history of the creation of aristocratic Southern culture and both its gallantry and tragic defeat in the Civil War.

The next day Ellen Fairchild's encounter with the mysterious girl in James's Bayou widens out beyond its first casual appearance, to transform ordinary reality into an eternal religious moment. The densely tangled woods where Ellen walks seem a cathedral of vines and passion flowers and the last remnants of the defeated Choctaw Indian culture.

> Moss from the cypresses hung deep overhead now, and by the water vines like pediments and arches reached from one tree to the next. . . . The cypress trunks four feet thick in the water's edge stood opened like doors of tents in Biblical engravings. How still the old woods were. Here the bayou banks were cinders; they said it was where the Indians burned their pottery, at the very last (*DW*, pp. 68–9).

To Ellen 'it seemed an ancient place and for a moment the girl was not a trespasser but someone who lived in the woods, a dark creature not hiding, but waiting to be seen, careless on the pottery bank'. Ellen tells the girl that she had been looking for the garnet pin she had lost, but as Ellen begins to represent 'a mother to all the world' in the deepening mystery of the encounter, the lovely girl assumes the role of the eternal daughter, whose sexuality is symbolised by the rose-shaped garnet pin Ellen's husband Battle had given her during their courtship. In the mythic traditions of Demeter, the Kore figure is the maiden manifestation of the great goddess, and Hecate is the aged crone. Thus it is not really strange that the mysterious young woman can share the attributes of the mother when she asserts her freedom from Ellen's control. As the girl speaks, 'a half-smile, sweet and incredibly maternal, passed over her face. It made what she said seem teasing and sad, final and familiar, like the advice a mother is bound to give her girls' (*DW*, p. 71).

Later in the day we learn that this nameless Kore has somehow substituted for Ellen's daughters in bearing the consequences of the danger of rape and tragedy. In the evening Ellen confides to her brother-in-law about meeting the girl, and she is amazed to learn that George had met her too. George calmly explains, 'I took her over to the old Argyle gin and slept with her, Ellen.' Shocked and melancholy, sure now that George is miserable without Robbie, Ellen also realises that George has saved the family from some obscure threat.

She had feared for the whole family, somehow, at a time like this (being their mother, and the atmosphere heavy with the wedding and festivities hanging over their heads) when this girl, that was at first so ambiguous, and so lovely even to her all dull and tired – when she touched at their life, ran through the woods. She had not had a chance to face this fear before, for at the time she had to cope with the runaway girl herself, who was only the age of her daughter Dabney, so she had believed. But at last she was standing quietly in the long twilight with George, bitterly glad (now it was certain; he was not happy) that he had been the one who had caught the girl, as if she had been thrown at them; for now was it not over? (*DW*, p. 80).

After Dabney's wedding is successfully concluded, we learn with Ellen that 'it' had not yet been over. The photographer who has come down from Memphis to take the wedding pictures reports, between flashes from his camera, that his train had hit and killed a girl. The photographer has captured her body on film, as he is now capturing the bridal party. For Ellen this is 'a vision of fate; surely it was the young girl of the bayou woods that was the victim this man had seen' (*DW*, p. 218). By sleeping with her, George had symbolically made her the Persephone who disappears into the world of death and thus a sacrificial substitute for Dabney.

On the afternoon after Ellen's meeting with the bayou girl, Dabney's older sister Shelley, accompanied by India and Laura, conducts a symbolic trip into the underworld which restores another Kore-figure to the world of light and sets the stage for the solution of George's problem and the threat to Dabney's wedding. Shelley's ostensible mission is to do some shopping in town and visit old Partheny, who was midwife to Ellen during her first child's birth and who raised two generations of Fairchilds before she retired from duty. Partheny is a formidable old black woman of magic powers suggested by the origin of her name in the Greek word for virgin. The word is the root of 'parthenogenesis' and therefore suggests independent female reproductive power. Partheny functions as a Hecate figure dominating the female labyrinth. When Shelley and India and Laura enter Brunswick-town, the black residential neighbourhood, they seem to descend from the sunny road into a witches' cave, 'into the abrupt shade of chinaberry trees and fig trees'. The place is populated only by old women during the day and filled with the smells of scalding water, feathers, iron pots and darkness. 'A devious, invisible vine of talk seemed to grow from shady porch to shady porch, though all the women were hidden. The alleys went like tunnels under the chinaberry branches, and the pony cart rocked over their black roots' (*DW*, p. 128).

Partheny suddenly appears to her visitors, stepping out from behind the screen of thick butter-bean vines that protects her little house from curious eyes. She is 'taller than a man, flat, and narrow, the color of midnight-blue ink'. At the end of their visit, with a look of malignity, pride and authority, she gives Shelley a strange cake to take to George with orders to 'tell him mind he eat it tonight at midnight, by himself, and go to bed. Got a little white dove blood in it, dove heart, blood of a snake – things. . . . his love won't have no res' till her come back to him' (*DW*, p. 131).

Next the girls visit the graveyard and are introduced to the world of the dead by Charon-like Dr Murdoch, who has assisted at all the family births and deaths. Like Brunswick-town, the cemetery is shielded from ordinary life by vegetation. Here quiet and fragrant gloom is created by a dense wall of honeysuckle vines around the cemetery and big cedars and rosebushes inside among the graves. Laura is pierced by grief when she sees the new grave of her mother and remembers her lonely father back in Jackson. 'She tried to see her father coming home from the office. . . . If she could not think of that, she was doomed; and she was doomed, for the memory was only a flicker, gone now' (*DW*, p. 134). Life and death intermingle in this pastoral plantation world, as Laura suddenly realises among the remains of the dead, and she fears that she will lose her own reality in this timeless place.

The final episode of the underworld journey is the visit to the Fairchild store, a dim treasure-house of family bounty redolent with warm fragrances of food and suggestive of the riches of Pluton.

> The air was a kind of radiant haze, which disappeared into a dim blue among hanging boots above – a fragrant store dust that looked like gold dust in the light from the screen door. Cracker dust and flour dust and brown-sugar particles seemed to spangle the air the minute you stepped inside. . . . All was warm and fragrant here. The cats smelled like ginger when you rubbed their blond foreheads and clasped their fat yellow sides. Every counter smelled different, from the ladylike smell of the dry-goods counter with its fussy revolving ball of string, to the manlike smell of coffee where it was ground in the back. There were areas of banana smell, medicine smell, smells of feed, shot, cheese, tobacco, and chicory, and the smells of the old cane chairs creaking where the old fellows slept (*DW*, p.137)

Laura searches here for a present to give her Uncle George and declares, 'Nothing you have is good enough!' Little Pan-like Ranny cries, 'Nine, ten, a big fat hen!' and suddenly there is Robbie. It does not matter that she is weeping and angry. She has been found, and she is the only gift good enough for George. Robbie is a missing Kore, whose restoration to her Dionysian husband will ensure a propitious union for Troy and Dabney. In fact, just after Shelley and India and Laura have left the store, Troy appears there and gently persuades Robbie to go to Shellmound and find George. Troy will even stop her along the way and give her a bite of Partheny's magic patticake that has been given him by India and that he has already tasted. The charm begins to work, if only on a level of dramatic irony. The potentially dangerous, non-Fairchild member of each crucial young marriage has tasted the magic cake and is prepared to be united with the appropriate mate. Even

Pinchy, who has also tasted the patticake, seems affected. She has been acting distracted, even crazed, through the days of her 'coming through', but in the evening after she has tasted Partheny's cake, the servants cry out, 'Hallelujah! Hallelujah! Pinchy's come through!'

Robbie's return to Shellmound is a dangerous event, with its own ritual overtones, which brings the family problems to a crisis. She arrives angry, hot, and exhausted from her long midday walk across the blazing cotton fields, and George is not even there to meet her. As she stumbles into the family at dinner, she lets a bird into the house. That is an omen of death, as all the Fairchilds realise, jumping up from the table to chase it and leaving Ellen to confront the aggrieved Robbie. The bird is a female brown thrush, like Robbie a wild and shy creature, and her frantic beating against the walls and windows parallels Robbie's desperate struggles against entrapment in the Fairchild clan. If Robbie's anger cannot be tamed, George's happiness will be destroyed, and the hope it embodies for Dabney and Troy will be blasted. Ellen faces Robbie's accusations of Fairchild snobbishness, tries to quiet her grief over her separation from George, and then, when George appears in the door looking joyous to see his wife again, Ellen charges him with having made Robbie suffer. At that moment shouts from upstairs herald the bird's capture, and Ellen realises that danger has been barely averted. 'The Yellow Dog had not run down George and Maureen; Robbie had not stayed away too long; Battle had not driven Troy out of the Delta; no one realized Aunt Shannon was out of her mind; even Laura had not cried yet for her mother. For a little while it was a charmed life' (*DW*, p. 166). Then Ellen faints in relief.

During the ensuing turmoil of wedding preparations and the very public reconciliation of George and Robbie, Laura and her cousin Roy slip away to visit Marmion. What follows is a dual ritual, blessing the old mansion and symbolically initiating Roy and Laura into puberty.

Marmion is a beautiful house, 'an undulant tower with white wings at each side, like a hypnotized swamp butterfly', but it was blighted by tragedy just after it was built and has stood empty for more than thirty years. The evil spell is removed in a fertility ritual performed by another black matriarch, crotchety old Aunt Studney, who always carries a huge sack believed by the Fairchild children to be the source of babies. Laura and Roy come upon the old woman as she is entering the deserted house with her sack. Aunt Studney stands in the middle of the tower room, hovering over her sack like a bird over an egg, while Roy runs round and round, up the spiral staircase of the tower, and Laura plays notes on a little 'fairy' piano. All at once Aunt Studney makes 'a cry high and threatening like the first note of a song at a ceremony, a wedding or a funeral, and like the bark of a dog too, somehow' (*DW*, p. 176). Suddenly the place is alive with bees.

These insects have a long history of association with feminine fertility, for their highly organised communities are ruled by a powerful queen, they serve the pollenating office necessary to the reproduction of many plants and they make a food that has always been considered a pure sign of nature's bounty. The tower room at Marmion, where the bees seem to swarm from Aunt Studney's womblike sack, has been described earlier in the book as having a chandelier 'chaliced, golden in light, like the stamen in the lily down-hanging' (*DW*, p. 122). This flower image appears again when Aunt Studney performs her ritual. 'Out of the tower's round light at the top, down by a chain that looked the size of a spider's thread, hung the chandelier with its flower-candles' (*DW*, p. 175). Once we realise that the room itself is a kind of flower, we understand that Eudora Welty intended Aunt Studney's ceremony to be a kind of pollenation that prepares for a new flowering of life in the old house.

Roy's ascent of the tower has clearly sexual overtones.

At the climactic moment when Aunt Studney makes her strange cry, Roy crows from the top of the tower, 'Troy! Troy! Look where I am! . . . I see the whole creation! Look, look at me, Papa!' As if to mark his phallic achievement, a bee stings Roy at the nape of his neck. Then as he and Laura are leaving Marmion they share a discovery which unites them temporarily as initiates in Aunt Studney's magic.

Laura finds a jewelled pin that looks like a rose, the very one her Aunt Ellen had been searching for when she met the beautiful girl in the bayou woods. Shaped like the flower traditionally identified with feminine beauty, the pin represents feminine sexuality even more obviously than the brooch Minta Doyle loses in *To the Lighthouse*. It had been Battle Fairchild's courtship gift to Ellen, now appropriately rediscovered by her niece who is on the brink of puberty. Laura does not keep it long, however. During the boat ride back to Shellmound, Roy suddenly throws his cousin into the Yazoo River. 'As though Aunt Studney's sack had opened after all, like a whale's mouth, Laura opening her eyes head down saw its insides all around her – dark water and fearful fishes' (*DW*, p. 178). The garnet pin is lost again, this time in the fertile waters of the Yazoo.

Roy pulls his cousin up by the hair, gets her back in the boat, and then explains that he 'thought girls floated'. 'You sure don't know much,' says Laura. Neither of them knows much about the rituals from which they have just emerged. Together the eight-year-old boy and the nine-year-old girl have attended a pollenation ceremony, Roy supplying masculine vitality and Laura sounding the magic note on the little piano while Aunt Studney releases the bees. Together they have discovered the jewelled feminine talisman in the grass, and then Laura has been immersed in the Yazoo River, whose name means River of Death. The imagery likening the water to Aunt Studney's sack makes it clear that the river is also the womb of life. Laura's baptism is more than an introduction to this mysteriously erotic element. It cleanses the taint of her mother's recent death so that she can participate in Dabney's wedding without threatening its hopeful tone.

Dabney's wedding day dawns auspiciously, and the final ceremonial preparations are capped by the arrival of both Negro matriarchs. Aunt Studney appears like an omen in the kitchen and then mysteriously disappears. Partheny materialises at the head of the stairs, 'clothed from top to bottom in purple' just in time to array the bride. 'She went straight and speaking to nobody to Dabney's closed door and flung it open. "Git yourself here to me, child. Who dressin' you? Git out, Nothin'," and Roxie, Shelley and Aunt Primrose all came backing out. The door slammed' (*DW*, p. 210).

Little space is devoted to the wedding itself, because that ritual is practically a cliché and an anticlimactic end to the drama of preparation. Welty simply tells us that 'Mr Rondo married Dabney and Troy'. But the visual symbolism of the wedding tableau rounds out the pastoral and mythic associations that have hovered about the event from the beginning. The bridesmaids all carry shepherds' crooks bedecked with flowers and are themselves dressed in the colours of roses, fading from American Beauty red at the two sides farthest from the bride to pale pink nearest her. Dabney wears pure white, of course, and her Aunt Tempe thinks that she looks dead, like all brides (*DW*, p. 214). Into this dainty pastoral scene Troy like the dangerous fiery god of the underworld, 'came in from the side door, indeed like somebody walking in from the fields to marry Dabney. His hair flamed' (*DW*, p. 213).

The harvest moon rises on the dance after the wedding and the bride and groom drift away into the night. Between their departure and return to Shellmound, Welty describes the family's recovery from the festivities in terms that emphasise fertility and childbirth. Just after the wedding, while guests circulate through the house eating cake and

dancing, Ellen tells the story of the birth of her first child,
Shelley. It had seemed almost parthenogenic, because it was
attended solely by women. Ellen's own mother had come
from Virginia to be with her, and Dr Murdoch had fallen
victim to his new anaesthesia machine so that Partheny had
had to deliver the baby. In a final emphasis on the theme
of birth, Laura remembers a stocking doll her own mother
had made her one summer day, a spontaneous gift from
mother to daughter, again suggesting feminine control
over reproduction. The doll is named 'Marmion' and thus
associated with the Delta and the house where Troy and
Dabney will take up their life together.

The morning after the wedding Ellen rises ahead of
the rest of her family to tend her thirsty and battered
garden. Her attachment to her flowers recalls Mrs Ramsay's
similar concerns but also clearly links childbirth and family
to the cultivation of her roses, petunias, dahlias, camelias,
hyacinths and abelias with their polleny bumblebees and
butterflies and birds (*DW*, pp. 224–5).

Delta Wedding ends with a family picnic three days
after the wedding, in which the whole extended family is
reunited on the grounds of Marmion with the newly-married
couple, just back from their honeymoon in the exotic nether
world of New Orleans. Persephone has been restored to
her mother, and a new vitality stirs in the family. Ellen
will soon have her baby, and the younger generation of
women represented by both Robbie and Dabney will begin
childbearing as well. The Delta landscape is as magical this
final night as it was in the opening pages of Laura's arriving
vision. Here it forms the background for Ellen's musings on
the eternal cycles of fertility and their relation to her own
womanhood.

The night insects all over the Delta were noisy; a kind
of audible twinkling, like a lowly starlight, pervaded the
night with a gregarious radiance.

Ellen at Battle's side rode looking ahead, they were comfortable and silent both, with their great weight, breathing a little heavily in a rhythm that brought them sometimes together. The repeating fields, the repeating cycles of season and her own life – there was something in the monotony itself that was beautiful, rewarding – perhaps to what was womanly in her. . . .

They rolled on and on. It was endless. The wheels rolled, but nothing changed. Only the heartbeat played its little drum, skipped a beat, played again (*DW*, p. 240).

Husband and wife move together through the repeating cycles of life wherein the individual is only a momentary pulse-beat in a changeless rhythm.

Through much of the novel, Laura has yearned to belong to the Fairchild clan. Her wish is granted when her aunt Ellen invites her to stay at Shellmound after the wedding. At first Laura agrees with delight, but we have seen her frightened realisation in the cemetery that absorption in this Delta world would be a kind of doom, and she feels that 'in the end she would go – go from all this, go back to her father' in Jackson (*DW*, p. 237). In coming to this decision, Laura is not rejecting the maternal values that Shellmound represents. She has been initiated into them by being included in the epithalamion rituals, as we have seen, and her involvement allows her to absorb the feminine mysteries which sustain the family. In a symbolic sense, these are her inheritance from her Fairchild mother just as the doll Marmion is in a more palpable way. Having received her feminine inheritance, she can now return to her father and hold her own. Her response must be ours as readers. Like Laura we must leave the pastoral retreat and return to the modern urban world of work, time and pain, but as we do, we bear with us a knowledge of the healing powers of ancient feminine traditions. At the picnic India shares a secret with her cousin: 'I'm going to have another

little brother before long, and his name shall be Denis
Fairchild' (*DW*, p. 241). Denis will be reborn, and with
Laura we see that it has all happened before. The cycles
of renewal so vividly performed in the maternal garden will
continue to sustain hope when we return to ordinary human
experience.

Laura returns to her father, not only because the
patriarchal urban world is the norm of twentieth-century
experience, but also because it is deeply in need of
what women provide, and Laura senses this in her
father's life. The patriarchy has always rested upon
the support of women, though it has never seriously
acknowledged that dependence. Laura's fleeting vision of
her father in the Fairchild cemetery reveals her sympathy
for his vulnerability and dependence. Laura thinks in the
cemetery of how her father walks home from his office, with
nobody to watch for him now that her mother is dead and
she herself is away.

> She tried to see her father coming home from the
> office, first his body hidden by leaves, then his face
> hidden behind his paper. If she could not think of that,
> she was doomed; and she was doomed, for the memory
> was only a flicker, gone now (*DW*, pp. 133–4).

In Laura's mind, he ceases to exist without a loving
woman to watch his daily return from his office. As long
as his daughter can call this vision to her mind, he exists.
But in the graveyard where her mother lies with the other
dead Fairchilds, Laura cannot retain his image and knows
she has lost him unless she soon returns to Jackson. We
should also notice that she feels herself doomed if this
loss occurs, because her life somehow depends as much
on her relation to her father as his reality does on her
presence and attention. Welty is here affirming the need
for interdependence between male and female, as she does

throughout *Delta Wedding* with her emphasis upon marriage and Laura's experience with Roy at Marmion. The world of Shellmound rests on female power, but it exists in co-operation with the masculine; similarly, the father-centred world of Jackson requires the feminine.

Welty's treatment of the relation between Laura and her father is similar in certain respects to her demonstration of George's need for Robbie. Unlike the privileged gaze of male writers and their narrative personae, which typically objectifies female characters and freezes them into power-less stereotypes which serve the needs of the observer, the feminine gaze of *Delta Wedding* recognises the subjectivity of males. At the same time it acknowledges their need for relation with the feminine and assumes cooperation between male and female as a condition for human community.

Laura is not alone among the daughter-figures in *Delta Wedding* to move beyond the traditional maternal sphere. Attention to the portraits of Ellen Fairchild's various daughters reveals that they will not accept the traditional feminine roles performed by their mother and aunts. The mysterious Kore figure Ellen meets in the bayou woods ventures out too far from maternal protection and is killed on her way to the fleshpots of Memphis, but Ellen's own daughters will conduct their explorations with more moderation.

Dabney muses about her need to break out of the Fairchild family mould as she rides toward the Grove to visit her spinster aunts, and her definition of her independence is expressed in terms of the rebellious sexual mores of the 1920s. Dabney has defiantly chosen a husband from a lower social class, who grew up among the poor hill-people of northern Mississippi. Troy is her father's employee and someone her whole family sees as unsuitable. She feels that her Fairchild identity is a skin or shell that she is preparing to leave behind her with marriage, as do the locusts who leave their discarded shells on the trees she passes on her ride. This anticipation of her independent future causes her to fidget during her visit with her aunts, and to have the urge to break all the little antiques in their house. She bursts out with shocking answers to their prim questions, saying that she runs with a crowd of fast girls and dances barefooted all night. This exaggerated language identifies her with the 'flappers', or New Women, whose emancipated behaviour shocked polite society during the 1920s. When she arrives back at Shellmound, Dabney unconsciously abandons the heritage embodied in the china night-light which her aunts have tried to pass on to her. She sees Troy's silhouette in a lighted window as she dismounts, and as she runs impetuously into the house, she lets the little night-light fall and smash to pieces on the ground.

On her solitary morning ride across the plantation the day before her wedding, Dabney muses about the masculine traditions of honour represented by the house where she and Troy will take up their married life. Such traditions are encoded in the antebellum myths which previous generations of Southern women have supported, but Dabney is outraged at the waste and bloodshed they have caused.

Marmion had been empty since the same year it was completed, 1890 – when its owner and builder, her grandfather James Fairchild, was skilled in the duel he fought with Old Ronald McBane, and his wife Laura Allen died broken-hearted very soon, leaving two poor Civil War-widowed sisters to bring up the eight children. . . . Honor, honor, honor, the aunts drummed into their ears. . . . To give up your life because you thought that much of your *cotton* – where was love, even, in that? *Other* people's cotton. Fine glory! Dabney would not have done it (*DW*, p. 120).

Here Welty explicitly counters the kind of masculine 'chivalry' dramatised by William Faulkner in *Sartoris*, when he fictionalises a similar duel which cost his own great-grandfather's life at the hands of a former business partner. Such behaviour was supposed to be the gallant inheritance of Civil War heroes. By placing it in the clear-headed practical perspective of a young white woman, exactly the kind of pure young lady for whom the knights of the Lost Cause claimed they fought their war, Welty refutes its claims and concentrates instead on its disastrous results.

Dabney's sister Shelley rejects the traditional codes of her culture more subtly and profoundly than her younger sister. At the end of the novel, she is preparing to go to Europe with Aunt Tempe, leaving the scenes of her Delta girlhood far behind. Undoubtedly she will return for a time, but she has been defined as a person who will not settle into domesticity even to the extent that her impatient sister and aunt Robbie do. Shelley has been a tomboy, but at the same time she finds herself frightened of walking the railroad trestle with her brothers and sisters the day the Yellow Dog nearly kills George and Maureen. Emotionally cautious and serious, Shelley holds herself aloof, watching and analysing the actors in the family drama. As she speculates in her diary about her family, she performs the role of the writer who explores the motives and defines the meaning of the life around her. Her diary perceptively defines the terror surrounding the episode of the train almost running down George and Maureen, as she alone of all the family understands how deeply George and Robbie wounded each other that day.

While most Fairchilds cheerfully ignore trouble, Shelley broods about it. One night in particular, she blunders into an understanding of violence and pain which most of her family, and especially its women, never see. Because Troy is late for the rehearsal dinner, Shelley is sent to fetch him. She bursts into his office to find him sitting in starched white suit facing a tense group of field-hands who have been fighting. Three of the men are wounded,

124   EUDORA WELTY

and the fourth menaces Troy with an ice-pick. Shelley
has always known that Troy's job as overseer was to
control and direct the Negro plantation workers, but she
has only a vague sense of what this means because women
have always been shielded from the process. When Welty
wrote the novel in the 1940s, most white Southerners were
carefully protected from witnessing the masculine exercise
of the force required to maintain white supremacy, but since
the Civil Rights battles of the 1960s the whole United States,
and indeed, the rest of the world, has clearly understood its
dynamics. Troy's ability to control male violence is close to
George's and Battle's knowledge of the rage which bubbles
under the graceful surface of Southern life. It is an often
bloody reality, most closely associated with Negroes, from
which the men protect the matriarchal plantation world.

Shelley stands frozen in the midst of the confrontation
between blacks and their white overlord and watches Troy
calmly shoot the man who had been ready to throw the
pick at him. We learn that the fight Troy has stopped
had a sexual cause – Pinchy. 'Pinchy cause *trouble* comin'
through,' says one of the blacks to another as they carry the
wounded Root M'Hook out the door. Shelley must jump
over the blood on the doorsill in order to get out of the
office and back to the safety of the big house.

She has been introduced to the dark, bloody side of life
which Dabney knows nothing about. Surprisingly, Shelley's
main reaction is not fear. She stays icily calm through the
fight, and then, as she runs home along the bayou, she
grows angrier and angrier to think of the way men behave
among themselves. Her interrogation of masculine codes
of heroism is more profoundly deprecatory than Dabney's,
because Shelley sees it as mere childish imitation, having
no real substance.

Suppose the behavior of all *men* were actually no more
than this – imitation of other men. But it had previously

occurred to her that Troy was trying to imitate her father.
(Suppose her *father* imitated . . . oh, not he!) Then all
men could not know any too well what they were doing.
Everybody always said George was a second Denis.

> She felt again, but differently, that men were no better
> than little children. . . . Women, she was glad to think,
> did know a *little* better – though everything they knew
> they would have to keep to themselves . . . oh, forever!
> (*DW*, p. 196)

Shelley's rejection of the masculine code differs from
Dabney's in its analysis of ignorance and immaturity at its
core. Her suggestion that women must keep their superior
knowledge to themselves implies some essential barrier
between the sexes which is unfortunately never further
defined in the novel. If Shelley is correct, there seems
little hope that men can learn to change their behaviour.
Although she sides with the feminine values of peace and
life as Dabney does, Shelley realises at bedtime the night
of this unpleasant revelation that violence and horror are
essential components of life. 'There was a whirr and a
clawing at the window screen back of the light. A big
beetle, a horned one, was trying to get in. All at once
Shelley was sickeningly afraid of life, life itself, afraid
for life. . . . She turned out the light, fell on her bed, and
the beating and scratching ceased' (*DW*, p. 197). For the
Egyptians, as Welty surely knew, the beetle, or scarab, was
a symbol of the soul. Shelley senses the intimate connection
of human desire with the ugly creature's clawing efforts to
come into the light from the darkness, and she retreats from
the spectacle by turning off her light.

After the wedding, Shelley dances with George and
ponders her future. The cavorting movement of her
uncle's body transmits a sense of the excitement awaiting
her, though she realises 'she might not be happy either,
wholly, and she would live in waiting, sometimes in

terror'. Dabney's marriage has a finality that separates the
sisters' fates. Shelley's thoughts flee from contemplation of
Dabney's life with Troy, 'to an open place – not from one
room to another room with its door, but to an opening wood,
with weather – with change, beauty' (*DW*, p. 220). Whereas
Dabney's world will be one of domestic enclosures, Shelley's
will be figured forth in wilder terrains. Thus once again,
feminine assertion expresses itself in terms of movement
over wide landscapes.

Delta Wedding closes with the Fairchild family gathered
together at a picnic which initiates a new spirit of life in
the old plantation, but Shelley's imminent departure and
Laura's final gesture open our sense of possibility out, away
from the family locus centred on traditional motherhood,
and into the vast spaces of the universe. Laura has the
final word in the novel, claiming to know the destiny of a
shooting star that falls through the night sky, and opening
her arms to the whole mystery of 'the radiant night'.

5 New Women

Eudora Welty's final work of the 1940s, *The Golden Apples* and the last novel she has published to date, *The Optimist's Daughter*, both focus on modern daughters who venture out beyond the protected domestic precincts of traditional womanhood. These women are similar to the daughters of *Delta Wedding* in their testing and revising of prescribed roles. *The Golden Apples* presents several alternative solutions to the problem of redefining the possibilities of feminine identity by dramatising the growth from childhood to maturity of Cassie Morrison, Virgie Rainey, and Jinny Love Stark in the small town of Morgana, Mississippi. Welty places their development in the heterosexual context of small-town society where relationships of family, generation, sex, social class and race involve them in a complex web within which their individual choices must be defined. *The Optimist's Daughter* concerns the return of another such woman to her small Mississippi home town, after she has made a successful independent professional life for herself in the urban North. The illness and death of her elderly father is the occasion which brings her back to confront the meaning of her parents' lives. Through her grief she comes to a new understanding of her mother as the real centre of her family, and her mother's pain becomes the key to accepting the central loss in her own life. Both works proceed from an authorial gaze that is essentially defined by the experience of women but which is characteristically Welty's in its sympathetic inclusion of varieties of masculine subjectivity.

The Golden Apples belongs in the curiously American genre of short-story collection or cycle in which the parts are so closely related as to constitute a sort of loose novel. Sherwood Anderson's *Winesburg Ohio*, Ernest Hemingway's *In Our Time* and William Faulkner's *Go Down, Moses* are the best-known works in this category, and like them, Welty's *The Golden Apples* needs to be seen as a whole.

In *The Golden Apples* Welty returns to the kind of male vitalising and fertilising figures who intruded upon female spaces in *The Wide Net*. This time, however, they are ultimately contained within the bounds of the feminine. The stories alternate between essentially masculine subjects and feminine subjects, but male experience is always framed by feminine space and political power and perspective. The first and third stories, 'Shower of Gold' and 'Sir Rabbit', are about a Zeus-figure, the priapic King MacLain, who wanders in and out of the town and surrounding woods seducing women. The narrator of the 'Shower of Gold', however, is Katie Rainey, a disapproving woman whose gossipy voice dominates the story and who is the mother of the central female character of the whole collection. 'Sir Rabbit', the third story, is told from the point of view of a country girl whom King rapes in descriptive terms echoing Yeats's 'Leda and the Swan'. The long second and fourth stories, 'June Recital' and 'Moon Lake' concern a group of girls who even before puberty are beginning to define their relationship to socially prescribed female roles. 'Moon Lake' is followed by two stories focused on the sons of King MacLain, both of whom are defeated by the women they marry. The final story, 'The Wanderers', returns to Virgie Rainey, who is now a woman past forty. She has made a defiantly unconventional place for herself in the town but prepares to strike out alone for new regions after the death of her mother. Welty uses the funeral of Katie Rainey as the occasion to bring together and contrast the women who had been piano pupils together as girls in 'June Recital'. As the story ends, Virgie frees herself from old associations and prepares to launch into a new life.

Where *Delta Wedding* employed one central myth as structural and symbolic principle, *The Golden Apples* returns to the freer and more catholic mixture of folklore and mythological materials that characterized *The Wide Net*. Welty has said that she was drawn to the name Morgana 'because I always loved the conception of *Fata Morgana* – the illusory shape, the mirage that comes over the sea'. This name helped her define the dreamlike atmosphere that seemed to drift in from the cottonfields around the little Delta town (*CNVRS*, p. 88). 'Morgana' also suggests the Celtic triple goddess Morrigan, who wooed and fought the hero Cuchulain in the Irish epic, the *Tain*. The character of King MacLain can be seen as a comic son (Mac) of the hero (Cuchulain), as he and his sons woo and battle strong women characters who dominate the life of the town and share many of Morrigan's qualities.[1] Many commentators have discussed the relation of the title to Yeats's 'Song of the Wandering Aengus', parts of which are quoted by Cassie Morrison in 'June Recital'. Yeats's 'Leda and the Swan' provides an analogy for King MacLain's rape of Mattie Will Sojourner in 'Sir Rabbit', as we have seen. The title of the first story, 'Shower of Gold' recalls the story of Zeus impregnating Danae by coming to her as a shower of gold in her lap. Welty makes sure we notice the connection by having the story's narrator refer to Snowdie MacLain as looking 'like a shower of something had struck her, like she'd been caught out in something bright' after the tryst with her wayward husband which caused her to become pregnant with her twin sons. Some commentators have likened Snowdie herself to Snow White, though King MacLain is far from a traditional princely consort for her. The final story in the cycle makes explicit parallels between the myth of Perseus (himself the product of Zeus's visit to Danae) and the gift of musical genius which Virgie Rainey has refused to develop, in defiance of Miss Eckhart's passionate efforts. In all the interweavings of myth and folklore with the realistic surface of these stories, Welty is again attempting, as she had in *Delta Wedding*, to suggest that ordinary reality is fuller of mystery than most of us imagine. Myths become metaphors for the meanings hovering about our experience that our excessively 'scientific' orientation has obscured.

King MacLain may be the invigorating Zeus-figure who fathers numbers of children in the region, but he is not finally an independent figure of authority. We know him *only* from the accounts of women narrators throughout *The Golden Apples*; he never voices his own experience or has any responsibility in town life. In 'Shower of Gold' we are introduced to his antics by the gossiping voice of Katie Rainey, at once outraged and amused by his antics. This narrative persona is one of Eudora Welty's triumphs of colloquial idiom, as is evident in the following confiding passage in which she describes the birth of twin boys to King's albino wife Snowdie.

The twins come the first day of January. Miss Lizzie Stark – she hates all men, and is real important: across yonder's her chimney – made Mr Comus Stark, her husband, hitch up and drive to Vicksburg to bring back a Vicksburg doctor in her own buggy the night before, instead of using Dr Loomis here, and stuck him in a cold room to sleep at her house; she said trust any doctor's buggy to break down on those bridges. Mrs Stark stayed right by Snowdie, and of course several, and I, stayed too, but Mrs Stark was not budging and took charge when pains commenced. Snowdie had the two little boys and neither one albino. They were both King all over again, if you want to know it. Mrs Stark had so hoped for a girl, or two girls. Snowdie clapped the names on them of Lucius Randall and Eugene Hudson, after her own father and her mother's father (*CS*, p. 267).

Katie Rainey's narrative places women in firm command of this result of King's unexpected visit to his wife nine months previously, and even the gentle and acquiescent Snowdie is matrilineal in naming her sons. Her wayward husband is of course absent when his legitimate offspring are born, just as he is when his illegitimate children come into the world. King was thought to have drowned in the Big Black River, but various Morgana men on business trips to the state capitol in Jackson or over in Texas claim to have sighted him fleetingly. Indeed he is not dead, but when he returns to his wife several years later, an Oedipal drama is played out on Snowdie's front porch that drives him away again before she even knows he has come. As King prepares to knock on the screen door, his two little sons wearing Halloween costumes and roller skates charge out 'hollering "Boo!" and waving their arms up and down the way it would scare you to death, or it ought to, if you wasn't ready for them' (CS, p. 271). By skating circles around their astonished father and 'saying in high birdie voices, "How do you do, Mister Booger?"', they frighten him so badly that he flees, leaving them in sole possession of their house and their mother. All through the story, King is so infrequently present that he seems almost a figment of Katie Rainey's imagination.

The next story centred on King is 'Sir Rabbit', told from the perspective of Mattie Will Sojourner. She is a country girl whose first sexual experience is with King's twin boys when she and they are 15 years old. Mattie Will is far from a passive victim, however, for she sees the boys coming after her in the woods, associates them with the seductions of their legendary father and waits for them rather than running away. The three children tumble and wrestle together on the loamy earth, and when they have finished their erotic play, they share sticks of candy the boys have brought in a paper sack.

The second part of the story occurs several years later

when she is married to a dull country boy named Junior
Holifield. This time she is out in the woods with her
husband and a black man who are hunting, when King
himself appears. Junior is unable to keep his wife to himself;
he stumbles backwards over a fallen tree and knocks himself
out. Then of course King has his way with Mattie Will, but
as Ruth Vande Kieft puts it, 'King is more absurdly human
than supernaturally heroic'.[2] Mattie Will has regarded him
from a distance with a deprecating, practical gaze that
notices his plain thatch of biscuit-coloured hair, and his
'puckered face . . . like a little boy's, with square brown
teeth.' The legendary seducer is getting on in years, but
when he comes forward to claim his conquest, Mattie
Will is stunned by his erotic force: 'she staggered, he
had such grandeur, and then she was caught by the hair
and brought down as suddenly to earth as if whacked by an
unseen shillelagh'. The description which follows echoes the
language of Yeats's 'Leda and the Swan' as Welty writes
that 'he put on her, with the affront of his body, the affront
of his sense too' (CS, p. 338). Yet the heroic implications
of the Yeatsian allusion are undercut by their comic context
here. Zeus had engendered Trojan civilisation by his rape
of Leda, however tragic its destiny. No future civilisation
is likely to result from King's conjunction with Mattie Will
in Morgan's Woods, and Welty describes the aftermath of
the event in terms which restore King to the inert form of
a sleeping mortal. After the rape, Mattie Will wanders in
the woods and comes upon him sleeping at the base of a
tree. Once again she sees him as a mere mortal, in practical
terms which deflate the fabulous image he had assumed
when he seduced her. His body lies sprawled in sleep, 'all
those parts looking no more driven than her man's now,
or of any more use than a heap of cane thrown up by the
mill and left in the pit to dry' (CS, p. 340). Mattie Will is
drawn to the MacLains because of their sexual reputations,
first as an inexperienced girl curious about sex, and second

as the bored young wife of an unimaginative clown, but they provide her only minor adventures in an otherwise unremarkable life. Welty seems to have used the inflated terms of myth to suggest King's erotic magnetism, but this force only temporarily interrupts an otherwise practical female intelligence.[3]

'June Recital' comes between these stories about the appearances and disappearances of the unpredictable King MacLain, and it primarily concerns an eccentric German piano teacher and her relationship with a gifted but rebellious girl who is her pupil. Narrative method is complex here, for the story begins as the observation of strange rituals in the deserted MacLain house by a bedridden 10-year-old boy next door, but it soon shifts into the mind of his older sister as she watches from her window and recalls a time some years earlier when she and other girls her age took piano lessons from Miss Eckhart in the same house. Perspective in this longest story in the cycle is thus essentially feminine, shifting back and forth from present activities in the delapidated house, to the past era when the house was the busy scene of piano lessons and the annual June recital as well as the lives of Snowdie and her boys.

The MacLain house is the literal focus of both Loch Morrison's and his sister Cassie's gaze on the summer day when Virgie Rainey and a sailor make love on a broken bed upstairs while downstairs an old man sleeps in one room and the now-demented Miss Eckhart festoons her former recital room with newspapers in preparation for setting the house afire. Loch and Cassie peer out of the windows of their bedrooms upon these increasingly bizarre and disturbing activities occurring in a place marked by disappointment and pain. Snowdie's desertion by her husband King had been compounded by the humiliation of having to take in boarders to earn her living, and Miss Eckhart had lived an embittered life with her elderly mother as an alien in the provincial Southern society of Morgana. Nevertheless, the old house is fuller of energy than the quiet and comfortable Morrison house next door. If it has been a site of disappointment, it has also been a place of passion represented by Miss Eckhart's devotion to music, especially that of Beethoven. Sixteen-year-old Cassie Morrison senses the strange energies of the deserted house next door and finds them disturbing.

Ever since the MacLains had moved away, that roof had stood (and leaked) over the heads of people who did not really stay, and a restless current seemed to flow dark and free around it . . . , a life quicker than the Morrisons' life, more driven, probably. . . . (CS, p. 286).

We learn in later stories that the appearance of middle-class stability and comfort in the Morrison house next door is deceptive, for problems beneath the surface of the Morrisons' lives lead Cassie's and Loch's mother to commit suicide. In the final story of the cycle, 'The Wanderers', we learn that order and respectability have been maintained at great cost in the household, for both Cassie and her father end up existing in pinched and diminished circumstances there, with the father reduced to the same occupation of looking at the world through a telescope from his bedroom window that his boy had been forced into by illness so many years before.

The dramatic core of 'June Recital' is the passionate relationship between Miss Eckhart and her most gifted pupil, young Virgie Rainey. Both of these women have returned to the MacLain house on the summer day when Loch and Cassie watch them from next door, but they are unconscious of each other's presence and of the way they are playing out the last tragicomic scene of their influence on each other's lives. As readers we learn what their actions signify, through Cassie Morrison's recollections of her and Virgie's childhood days when their musical instruction was administered by the frightening German spinster.

Miss Eckhart had been devoted to the most rigorous standard of professional musicianship, and it was clear from her dedication and sophistication that she had had a serious career before she unaccountably appeared in Morgana. There, however, she and her invalid mother lived a severely reduced existence as boarders in Miss Snowdie's house, supported by Miss Eckhart's giving piano lessons to the daughters of the town's polite citizens. The children think her studio is 'like the witch's house in *Hansel and Gretel*', and in its midst the heavy, ageless piano teacher sits beside her pupils with a flyswatter ready to smack their hands when they make mistakes. She is Germanically methodical and relentless, except where Virgie Rainey is concerned. Virgie's extraordinary musical gift is the one joy in Miss Eckhart's bleak life, and it prompts uncharacteristic smiles. ' "Virgie brings me good luck!" Miss Eckhart used to say, with a round smile on her face' (*CS*, p. 291).

Virgie Rainey is as wild and independent as she is talented. At 10 or 12 she has masses of dark, silky curls and is 'full of the airs of wildness'. To the other children she is as exciting as a gypsy, but 'Virgie's air of abandon that was so strangely endearing made even the Sunday School class think of her in terms of the future'. She seemed certain to leave Morgana and become a missionary or the first lady governor of Mississippi. To the timid and conventional Cassie, Virgie looked like a heroine from her *St Nicholas Magazine*.

She often took the very pose of that inventive and persecuted little heroine who coped with people she thought were witches and ogres (alas! they were not) – feet apart, head aslant, eyes glancing up sideways, ears cocked; but you could not tell whether Virgie would boldly interrupt

her enemies or run off to her own devices with a forgetful
smile on her lips (*CS*, pp. 291–2).

Cassie is perceptive in seeing Virgie's heroism, but she is
mistaken in belittling the forces against which Virgie sets
herself. The Raineys are barely acknowledged as members
of Morgana's middle class, as Cassie's mother makes clear
in condescending remarks about the family's finances and as
we also see in the schoolchildren's deprecating assumptions
that Virgie's hair is curly and luxuriant because it is dirty.
Virgie's father peddles buttermilk through the town, and
her mother sells ice cream at outdoor political speeches,
so that the children call her Miss Ice Cream Rainey. In
defiance of her classmates' taunting, Virgie drinks her
mother's vanilla ice-cream flavouring out of the bottle
and brags about it. Much of Virgie's wildness can be
seen as her proud refusal to be defined by the town's
smug standards.

Virgie's differences from the other girls her age –
her poverty and unconventionality and passion – are all
qualities she shares with Miss Eckhart, as well as her
gift for music. Miss Eckhart eats strange German foods
in her rented room and lives by a code incomprehensible
to Morgana. One day during a thunderstorm, she reveals
her romantic temperament to the frightened girls who
have never suspected that such violence lies beneath her
Teutonic regimen. She begins performing a piece of music
in tune with the thunder outside, and her face changes
into 'the face a mountain could have, or what might be
seen behind the veil of a waterfall'. The music makes all
the pupils uneasy, for it seems to flow 'like the red blood
under the scab of a forgotten fall'. Most unaccountably of
all, Miss Eckhart fails to comply with the local definition
of pure Southern womanhood, when she refuses to be
seriously discomfited after being raped by a black man.
The townspeople consider this the ultimate disgrace and

expect her to leave town for ever. Instead, she continues her life as if nothing has happened. 'It was because she was from so far away, at any rate, people said to excuse her . . . Miss Eckhart's *differences* where why shame alone had not killed her and killed her mother too' (*CS*, pp. 300–302).

Virgie is similarly independent in the way she eats and in her behaviour. She invents exotic sandwiches to take to school and conducts herself according to her own fierce motives.

> She would ride over on a boy's bicycle (her brother Victor's) from the Raineys' with sheets of advanced music rolled naked (girls usually had portfolios) and strapped to the boy's bar which she straddled, the magnolia broken out of the Carmichaels' tree and laid bruising in the wire basket on the handlebars. Or sometimes Virgie would come an hour late, if she had to deliver the milk first, and sometimes she came by the back door and walked in peeling a ripe fig with her teeth; and sometimes she missed her lesson altogether. . . .

> Virgie carried in the magnolia bloom like a hot tureen, and offered it to Miss Eckhart, neither of them knowing any better: magnolias smelled too sweet and heavy for right after breakfast (*CS*, pp. 289–90).

Cassie Morrison makes an effective narrator here, because her conventional view of her sex alerts us to the way both the magnolia bloom and the boy's bicycle signal Virgie's refusal to accept stereotypical 'feminine' standards. The rich white blossom has traditionally been identified with white Southern womanhood, and Virgie steals it from a neighbour's tree, handles it roughly, and offers it to the one woman in town who seems a strong enough model for her. The blossom's delicate, creamy whiteness is bruised as it bounces along in Virgie's careening bicycle, but Virgie's treatment of it seems nevertheless to suggest the speed and energy with which femininity can be borne. Virgie's rolling her music 'naked' around the phallic bar of the boy's bicycle and then straddling it as she rides wildly to her lesson suggests an open acceptance of sexuality that is closely connected to her musical talent.

Virgie's sexuality and the defiant way she bears her family's social position cause her to disappoint Miss Eckhart's hopes for the full development of her talent. They mark her as Miss Eckhart's mirror-image, a person with similar qualities but one who chooses a reverse pattern for deploying them. Miss Eckhart has disciplined her whole life around her musical vocation, and her sexual life is so stunted that its only expression is a pitifully shy and unfulfilled infatuation with a local shoe-salesman. Her appreciation for Virgie's talent is a touching gratitude in her otherwise emotionally barren life, and it puts Virgie in control of their relationship. Cassie Morrison tells us that Miss Eckhart 'gave all her love to Virgie Rainey and none to anybody else' (*CS*, p. 307). Even though she comes late for lessons and shows no deference to her teacher, when Virgie sits down to play, she always performs firmly and smoothly, advancing to more and more difficult music as the years go by. At the same time, however, she is steadily humiliating her teacher. The first step in this process of destruction comes when Virgie refuses to play to Miss Eckhart's precious metronome, insisting on setting her own rhythms. 'Miss Eckhart had made an exception of Virgie Rainey; she had first respected Virgie Rainey, and now fell humble before her impudence'. As time goes by, Virgie's manners grow worse and worse. 'Anybody could tell that Virgie was doing something to Miss Eckhart. She was turning her from a teacher into something lesser. And if she was not a teacher, what was Miss Eckhart?' (*CS*, pp. 293–4).

Virgie wins the battle of wills with her teacher, for

she simply stops studying the piano on her fourteenth birthday, about the same time that her brother Victor is killed in France in the First World War. Cassie Morrison, as narrator, seems unsure of Virgie's motives because she lacks the independence of mind to project herself into a consciousness like Virgie's. Most critics have assumed that Virgie acts out of perversity and the desire to destroy Miss Eckhart, but her abandonment of musical training could just as easily have been caused by financial problems which the immature and sheltered narrator would not understand. The Raineys' barn had been blown away some time before, and there had been no more money for lessons. Miss Eckhart had continued to teach Virgie free, but the time was obviously at hand when Virgie would have to help support her family. Cassie realises that Virgie had moved directly from puberty to adulthood, leaving her childhood companions behind in adolescence.

Virgie Rainey had gone straight from taking music to playing the piano in the picture show. With her customary swiftness and lightness she had managed to skip an interval, some world-in-between where Cassie and Missie and Parnell were, . . . Virgie had gone direct into the world of power and emotion . . . (CS, pp. 302–303).

Virgie now seems to Cassie to inhabit the romantic realm of the film stars whose screen adventures she accompanies on the piano at the local theatre. In fact, Virgie is next-door making love to a sailor while Cassie plays adolescent games and thinks of romance in the terms of motion-picture images. Her precocious entry into adult sexuality was symbolically prefigured by her appearance at her final triumphant recital when she was 13. The recitals always occurred in June, and all Miss Eckhart's pupils were required to dress as if for a wedding. All-female Morgana attended the festivity in a sweltering room full of flowers and paper streamers. Virgie performed in a white dress with a red sash, and 'when she finished and got up and made her bow, the red sash was all over the front of her waist, she was wet and stained as if she had been stabbed in the heart, and a delirious and enviable sweat ran down from her forehead and cheeks and she licked it in with her tongue' (CS, p. 313). Virgie's triumph is orgasmic, and she accepts its sensuous pleasure as naturally as she will soon accept sexual love.

Miss Eckhart's fortunes begin to decline with the defection of her star pupil, and she ends up living out in the country with a farming family in destitution. It is three years after Virgie's final recital when Cassie and Loch watch the old woman return to the scene of these former days, unaware that Virgie is upstairs cavorting naked with her lover. When Miss Eckhart sets her studio afire, a sequence of broad comedy occurs, involving two bungling old men who climb in a window to stop her, a now-shabby King MacLain who suddenly arrives to view the scene and then disappear, Virgie and the sailor who run out of the front door to escape, and the polite ladies of the neighbourhood who are just leaving a card-party in time to see the whole thing. Virgie and her young man run out of the house into a virtual wall of astonished feminine rectitude. 'Look at that!' one lady cries, 'I see you, Virgie Rainey!' Virgie simply stalks down the sidewalk calmly clicking her high heels 'as if nothing had happened in the past or behind her, as if she were free, whatever else she might be' (CS, p. 325). The ladies watch in a sudden hush, clutching their parasols. Then Virgie passes Miss Eckhart on the sidewalk, where two men are leading the old woman away. Cassie muses late that night, about the strange confrontation between the former teacher and her gifted pupil, now both embarked on other, sadder paths.

They were deliberately terrible. They looked at each other and neither wished to speak. They did not even

horrify each other. No one could touch them now,
either. . . .

Both Miss Eckhart and Virgie Rainey were human beings
terribly at large, roaming on the face of the earth. And
there were others of them – human beings, roaming, like
lost beasts (*CS*, p. 330).

Cassie's mind cannot support such a vision for long, and
she drifts into a dreamlike state in which Yeats's 'Song of
the Wandering Aengus' flows through her head. What she
does not understand is that both Virgie and Miss Eckhart
will continue to wander beyond the confines of conventional
existence, in search of 'the silver apples of the moon, the
golden apples of the sun', however terribly isolated their
determination may leave them. Yeats's poem describes the
mortal man in Celtic mythology who yearns for the love of
a fairy woman and for the life of beauty beyond the ordinary
world in which she exists. Cassie Morrison unconsciously
connects the poem with the events she has witnessed, but
she is not brave enough to accept the poem's lesson except
in dreams where she encounters the 'grave, unappeased,
and radiant face' of Yeats's wanderer. Virgie Rainey and
Miss Eckhart, in contrast, are themselves the very types
of that wanderer, and they accept the cost of the quest.[4]
In the final story of *The Golden Apples*, Virgie's pride and
Miss Eckhart's defeat come together and are resolved in the
image of Perseus and Medusa.

'Moon Lake', coming after the frank story of a country
girl's sexual initiation in 'Sir Rabbit', concerns the more
indirect initiation of a whole camp-full of pubescent girls
from more privileged families. The camp is a female preserve for one week in summer, when several polite ladies
under the imperious direction of Miss Lizzie Stark (Mrs
Comus Stark) supervise a regimen of swimming, hiking,
crafts, singing, and campfire activities for a crowd of
girls around 11, 12 and 13 years old that includes Miss

Lizzie's spoiled daughter Jinny Love and her friend Nina
Carmichael as well as a group of orphans. The only males
in the camp are the son of the Negro cook, and the white
lifeguard, Loch Morrison, both of them about the same
age as the girls. Point of view is that of the character,
Easter, who is the leader of the orphans and much like
Virgie Rainey in her hardy independence.

As in *Delta Wedding*, water is associated with sexuality,
and the tangled swampy growth around the lake is also an
erotic natural place similar to the bayou and the whirlpool at
Shellmound. Dewy trees in the early morning are 'weighted
with dew, leaning on one another's shoulders and smelling
like big wet flowers', and Welty connects them explicitly
with the girls, who prepare for swimming by walking out
of their kimonos and dropping them 'like the petals of one
big scattered flower' on the bank (*CS*, p. 343). The name
'Moon Lake' comes from an actual place in the Mississippi
Delta, but Welty seems to have chosen it especially for the
feminine traditions surrounding the moon and its close
associations with menarche and female reproductive cycles.
The water of the lake is entered forcefully by the women
counsellors but only hesitatingly by the girls. The orphans
are especially afraid of the water because they cannot
swim. The young counsellor, Miss Parnell Moody, uses
the moonlit lake for courtship, rowing out upon it with
her suitors to 'spoon'.

Loch Morrison despises all the girls and considers his
stint as Boy Scout lifesaver a martyrdom. He keeps himself
apart from their activities and only swims in the lake 'at
the hours too hot for girls'; then he states his masculinity
by diving from a high crosspiece in a big oak where the
men from the American Legion dive. His movements are
violent, rough, and determined: 'He went through the air
rocking and jerking like an engine, splashed in, climbed
out, spat, climbed up again, dived off' (*CS*, p. 34). He and
the girls may despise each other, but they are destined to

come together both in the camp and in their approaching adulthood, and the boy's crude energies will be lifesaving indeed.

Easter is the girl whom Loch will save in the story's climactic scene, but when we first see her, there seems little chance that she will need his services. When she is in the water, she stares at him with an unblinking gaze: 'At the other end of her gaze the lifesaver grew almost insignificant' (*CS*, p. 345). Her hair is cropped and wiry, and she is a tough, fearless tomboy who runs barefoot through the swampy woods and plays a mean game of mumblety-peg with her jack-knife. But she is also a girl on the brink of womanhood, as the orphans' benefactor, Mr Nesbitt from the Bible Class, recognises when he stares at her budding breasts. Her response is to bite his hand. Easter's eyes suggest the ancient female qualities she possesses, qualities which have nothing in common with the prissy daintiness of the girls from 'nice' families.

Easter's eyes, lifting up, were neither brown nor green nor cat; they had something of metal, flat ancient metal, so that you could not see into them. . . . The color in Easter's eyes could have been found somewhere, away — away under the lost leaves — strange as the painted color of the ants. Instead of round black holes in the center of her eyes, there might have been women's heads, ancient (*CS*, pp. 347–8).

When she describes her origins and destiny to answer Jinny Love and Nina's curiosity, she portrays herself as a completely female-identified person. 'I haven't got no father. I never had, he ran away. I've got a mother. When I could walk, then my mother took me by the hand and turned me in [to the orphanage], and I remember it. I'm going to be a singer' (*CS*, p. 358). Easter feels fully in control of her identity, for when she and Nina and Jinny

Love are exploring a deserted little strip of lakefront one day and writing their names in the sand, Easter renames herself 'Esther'. Jinny Love is characteristically insensitive and conventional in her assertion that 'Easter's just not a real name. It doesn't matter how she spells it, . . . nobody ever had it. Not around here.' Easter is firm. 'I have it' (*CS*, p. 357), she says, and in claiming her name(s), she associates herself with the dying and rising maiden spring-deity like Persephone in many cultures, and also with Esther, the Jewish queen of Persia who saved her people from massacre in the Old Testament.

In a passage describing the night as a mysterious male presence outside the girls' tent, Welty suggests Easter's openness to experience, particularly that associated with the masculine. 'The pondering night stood rude at the tent door, the opening fold would let it stoop in – it, him – he had risen up inside. Long-armed, or long-winged, he stood in the center where the pole went up.' The erotic connotations of this description are fairly obvious as the phallic night enters through the vaginal fold of the tent and rises up inside. Most of the girls draw back away from this presence in their sleep, but

> the night knew about Easter. . . . Easter's hand hung down, opened outward. Come here, night, Easter might say, tender to a giant, to such a dark thing. And the night, obedient and graceful, would kneel to her. Easter's callused hand hung open there to the night that had got wholly into the tent (*CS*, pp. 361–2).

In the story's climax, one of the camp's two boys, black Exum, causes Easter to fall into the lake from the diving board, and the other boy saves her from drowning. The Negro male and the white Boy Scout could thus be said to collaborate in the girl's symbolic immersion in the erotic watery element. The broad outlines of the event are reminiscent of Laura McRaven's similar near-drowning in the Yazoo River in *Delta Wedding*, caused by a boy who pulls her out of the water after pushing her in. Patricia Yaeger has alerted us to the imagery of rape which Welty uses to describe Loch Morrison's resuscitation of Easter on this last day of the camp.[5] As he heaves himself up and down on the prostrate girl's body, Loch horrifies all the feminine onlookers. Miss Lizzie Stark exercises her authority as Camp Mother in ordering Loch to stop and in seeming to reduce him 'almost to a nuisance – a mosquito, with a mosquito's proboscis' with her disapproving gaze. But Loch is relentless, and we must understand that he is a much more serious and necessary presence than she will admit.

> Easter's body lay up on the table to receive anything that was done to it. If *he* was brutal, her self, her body, the withheld life, was brutal too. While the Boy Scout, as if he rode a runaway horse, clung momently to her and arched himself off her back, dug his knees and fists into her and was flung back careening by his own tactics, she lay there (*CS*, p. 336).

Welty is explicit about the connection between the watery element of the lake which has almost killed Easter, and the masculine night in her tent the night before. As Loch pumps away on her back, Easter's arm dangles from the table at an angle that causes her hand to lie open as it did in her sleep, 'the same as it had held when the night came in and stood in the tent. . . . It was the one hand, and it seemed the one moment' (*CS*, p. 369). Easter seems to naturally accept the intertwined mysteries of night, death, sex and life as her inert body lies beneath Loch's cruel insistence that she begin to breathe again.

Patricia Yaeger argues that Easter is betrayed by these attentions and that 'Welty has created the cruelest possible entry into the world of sexuality for her characters; she has created a situation requiring protest that admits no protestation, for to rebel against Loch's ministrations would be to rebel against life itself.'[6] It is clear that here, as in 'At the Landing', Welty identifies brutal male sexuality with life itself, but Easter is not defeated by her initiation. Her body is only described as betrayed in the eyes of the other girls, when she lies apparently dead on the table. These girls consider her tricked by Exum's tickling her heel and thus frightening her into jumping off the diving board. But they are mistaken in believing this 'betrayal' final. In the act of reviving, Easter kicks the Boy Scout, who tumbles ridiculously backwards off the table. He falls into Miss Lizzie Stark and she collapses into a heap on the ground. The potentially tragic event has turned into comedy, and Easter sits up by herself, exhausted but once more in command of her life. 'Carry me,' she orders, and the other girls rush to her and carry her up to her tent.

'Moon Lake' ends with Nina and Jinny Love's glimpse of Loch Morrison naked in his tent, and we have seen that they deprecate his phallic heroism.[7] Welty simultaneously credits Loch's accomplishments *and* refuses to grant him the authority which acts of courage customarily win in male texts. It is true as Patricia Yaeger maintains, that the feminine world of 'Moon Lake' is temporary and hedged about by masculine systems of power. Already on the last day of camp, Ran MacLain has arrived with his dogs as the vanguard of a party of hunters who will move into the camp when the women have gone. Nevertheless, in the context of the whole of *The Golden Apples*, the masculine is enveloped by, surrounded and defined by, the feminine, just as Loch Morrison has been in this story. The male is a necessary invader and energiser of female space, but Welty's picture of heterosexual life parallels the physical topography of the sex-act in which the male violently enters and vitalises but is contained by the feminine.

In the two stories which follow 'Moon Lake' both of

the formerly potent sons of King MacLain are depicted in adulthood as exiles from homes ruled by their wives. Ran has been cuckolded by his spoiled young wife, the former Jinny Love Stark, in 'The Whole World Knows'. In his anguish, he addresses pleas for help to his absent father. King MacLain can be understood by now to be a type of the aristocratic Southern gentleman somewhat like Don McInnis of 'Asphodel', and like him symbolic of the failure of the Southern patriarchy. Ran's pleas grow more and more desperate, but there is never any answer, never any manifestation of fatherly presence. By the end of the story, after Ran has bumbled an attempt at suicide and has caused the ruin of the country girl who saved him from it, he has given up hope for advice. Instead he wistfully asks his father and his brother whether they have found anything better in their wanderings than the misery of his life in Morgana.

'Father, I wish I could talk to you, wherever you are right now', the story begins. Unlike the absent King, Ran's mother Snowdie is very present in his life, as we see in the very next lines:

Mother said, *Where have you been, son?* – Nowhere, Mother. – *I wish you wouldn't sound so unhappy, son. You could come back to MacLain and live with me now.* – I can't do that, Mother. You know I have to stay in Morgana (*CS*, p. 375).

To return to his mother would mean a return to childhood dependency, but Ran finds no solution to his problems as an adult male in his father's example. In fact, *The Golden Apples* is a world without real fathers; its only responsible adults are women. Ran's mother-in-law Miss Lizzie Stark rules the family he has joined in marriage, and she ignores her daughter's infidelity, continuing to observe the social forms which mark her as the leading respectable lady of

Morgana. The sanest woman in town is Miss Perdita Mayo, a kindly older lady who urges Ran to forgive his wife.

> Randall, when are you going back to your precious wife? You forgive her, now, you hear? That's no way to do, bear grudges. Your mother never bore your father a single grudge in her life, and he made her life right hard. I tell you, how do you suppose he made her life? She don't bear him a grudge. We're all human on earth (*CS*, p. 376).

This woman's tolerance emphasises the injustices of the traditional double standard which allows sexual freedom to men but denies it to women. She proposes an equal rule of tolerance for the weaknesses of both sexes, and it seems to be the standard that prevails in Morgana. By the final story of the cycle, we find Ran and Jinny reunited, parents of two children who will take their places in Morgana's new generation.

Eugene wanders all day through San Francisco in 'Music from Spain' after a quarrel with his wife Emma, seeking adventure with a Spanish guitarist he and Emma had recently seen in concert and whom he has chanced to meet on the street and decides to show the town. Like Leopold Bloom in Joyce's *Ulysses*, Eugene grieves for a dead child and spends his time away from his wife in rather desultory activities in his large city. By the end of the day he has spent his last penny and trudges home somewhat sheepishly. When he arrives, his wife is cheerfully engaged in conversation with a woman friend in the warm apartment full of the smell of hot chowder. He feels defeated by the women's self-sufficiency and knows that they will not be impressed by his having spent the day with the famous guitarist. Since his little daughter's death, he and Emma have drifted farther and farther apart, so that he is clearly not essential to her anymore. By the end of the cycle, Eugene is dead of tuberculosis, having returned alone to Morgana. There his 'light, tubercular body seemed to hesitate on the street of Morgana, hold averted, anticipating questions' (CS, p. 458). His wife only sent a telegram when he died.

'The Wanderers' take us full-circle in the cycle of stories, focusing on Katie Rainey's death and its effect on Virgie, who is a woman past 40 by this time. The story emphasises Virgie's essentially feminine identification and her continued independence. She had left Morgana for a time as a young woman but had returned to live with her mother. She remained as unpredictable as she had been in childhood, refusing to commit herself to any serious career or any person but her mother. To support herself she works steadily but only mechanically for a lumber company which ironically is destroying the woods that symbolise the natural energies motivating her. She continues to satisfy her physical needs outside of marriage with various men, one of whom often leaves a tribute of freshly shot quail on her doorstep. Her mother accepts her wayward daughter's habits, only fretting every afternoon that she will not get home in time to milk the cows. 'It's a wonder, though,' Mrs Rainey marvels when her daughter comes home each day on time. 'A blessed wonder to see the child mind' (CS, p. 430). Virgie would not show such consideration to anyone but her mother.

When Katie Rainey dies, Virgie confronts the loss of the only person who has had a just claim upon her life. The daughter performs a ritual the evening of the death which releases her from her lifelong ties to her mother but simultaneously reaffirms her essential unity with wider natural powers that Welty associates with the feminine – water and the moon.

> She stood on the willow bank. It was bright as mid-afternoon in the openness of the water, quiet and peaceful. She took off her clothes and let herself into the river.

> She saw her waist disappear into reflectionless water;
> it was like walking into sky, some impurity of skies.
> All was one warmth, air, water, and her own body. All
> seemed one weight, one matter – until as she put down
> her head and closed her eyes and the light slipped under
> her lids, she felt this matter a translucent one, the river,
> herself, the sky all vessels which the sun filled. She began
> to swim in the river, forcing it gently, as she would wish
> for gentleness to her body. Her breasts around which she
> felt the water curving were as sensitive at that moment as
> the tips of wings must feel to birds, or antennae to insects.
> She felt the sand, grains intricate as little cogged wheels,
> minute shells of old seas, and the many dark ribbons of
> grass and mud touch her and leave her, like suggestions
> and withdrawals of some ancient bondage that might
> have been dear, now dismembering and losing itself.
> She moved but like a cloud in skies, aware but only
> of the nebulous edges of her feeling and the vanishing
> opacity of her will, the carelessness for the water of the
> river through which her body had already passed as well
> as for what was ahead (*CS*, pp. 439–40).

This delicious baptism merges Virgie with a translucent
material reality in which water, sky, and her own body all
share the feminine shape of vessels filled by the sun. Welty
seems here to redefine the transcendent pastoral moment
in *Walden* when Thoreau floats in his little boat upon the
lake reflecting the sky and seeming to merge all nature
into peaceful harmony. Thoreau locates his male narrative
persona in a boat which protects his body from actual
contact with the lake and thus preserves physical distance
and autonomy. Virgie Rainey, in contrast, is fully immersed
in the watery element so that her body's outer layers become
surfaces of contact rather than separating boundaries. Her
relationship to the mystic unity of nature is not therefore a
cerebral imagining, as in Thoreau's masculine version, but

rather a full, bodily participation in the elements defining the material world outside the self. As Virgie moves gently through the water, the grains of sand and ribbons of watery plants 'touch her and leave her' like the bonds of her life with her mother, once dear but now dissolving away. Her own stubborn will seems to melt away with her ties to the past and her care for the future, and she is cleansed and prepared for the funeral she must endure the next day.

The funeral ceremonies bring Morgana society into the somewhat ramshackle Rainey house and involve Virgie in the kind of conventional public scenes which her eccentric way of life has generally spared her. Her former playmates, now the respectable married ladies of the town, observe the defiantly independent Virgie with disapproval because she has refused to accede to the narrow definitions of womanhood which have bound their lives. Former girlhood friends gather in the Rainey kitchen to cook the mounds of foods customary at funeral gatherings, but they stop what they are doing when Virgie comes into the room and stare at her 'as though something – not only today – should prevent her from knowing at all how to cook – the thing they knew' (CS, p. 434). It is an affront to their sense of righteousness that an 'abandoned' woman like Virgie should dare to practise the domestic arts of decent women. Jinny MacLain and Missie Spights both look disapprovingly at the burns and scars on Virgie's hands, 'making them stigmata of something at odds in her womanhood' because her very existence threatens their stereotyped notions of their sex. Jinny seems desperate, 'grimacing out of the iron mask of the married lady' in her efforts to drive everybody, 'even Virgie for whom she cared nothing, into the state of marriage along with her' (CS, pp. 444–5).

Surrounded by her mother's old friends, her own generation of Morgana's respectable citizens, and her mother's Mayhew relatives from the hill country, Virgie finds genuine personal sympathy only in the kindness of

Cassie Morrison, her girlhood rival in piano lessons. But an even keener alliance occurs unexpectedly between Virgie and the selfish old King MacLain, who has finally come home to stay. Before the burial, as the guests circulate and gossip around tables laden with hams and fried chicken, biscuits, cakes and pies, Virgie looks out from her mother's bedroom at the now shrivelled and obscene old King and shares a moment of recognition.

While Mamie C. Loomis, a child in peach, sang 'O Love That Will Not Let Me Go,' Mr King sucked a little marrow bone and lifted his wobbly head and looked arrogantly at Virgie through the two open doors of her mother's bedroom. . . . Mr King pushed out his stained lip. Then he made a hideous face at Virgie, like a silent yell. It was a yell at everything – including death, not leaving it out – and he did not mind taking his present animosity out on Virgie Rainey; indeed he chose her. Then he cracked the little bone in his teeth. She felt refreshed all of a sudden at that tiny but sharp sound (*CS*, p. 446).

Welty goes on to define more specifically the kinship Virgie recognises in this moment of alliance: 'it lacked future as well as past; but she knew when even [such] a rarified thing had become a matter of loyalty and alliance'. Both Virgie and King are determined to suck the marrow out of life and pay no attention to the pieties of small-town behaviour. King seems almost a spiritual father for Virgie, but unlike ordinary patriarchs who seek to control their daughters' actions, King treats Virgie as his equal and validates the independence they share by including her in his defiant grimace and in the affirmative act of cracking the little bone in his teeth.

After the funeral is over and Virgie has gone to bed, she is disturbed by an apparition recalling the restless yearnings she had expressed in music when she was young. These yearnings seem associated at once with the most basic animal needs and with wider feminine mysteries in maternal nature. She has known that the incoherent pain of her mother's cows calling to be milked is similar to the need she relieved by playing the piano. Through the long years of life with her mother, she has taken some comfort in using her talented fingers for milking these kindred female beasts. The cows are the very embodiment of female entrapment, domesticated and controlled to the point that they have become machines for making the maternal nourishment of milk constantly available to men. Even though Virgie has refused to accept the limits of human female domestication, she is nevertheless bound by the household routines of life with her mother and by the daily schedule of her clerical work in town. She identifies her own inarticulate pain with that of the cows, as she cramps her fingers daily in milking them.

> Her fingers set, after coming back, set half-closed; the strength in her hands she used up to type in the office but most consciously to pull the udders of the succeeding cows, as if she would hunt, hunt, hunt daily for the blindness that lay inside the beast, inside where she could have a real and living wall for beating on, a solid prison to get out of, the most real stupidity of flesh, a mindless and careless and calling body, to respond flesh for flesh, anguish for anguish. And if, as she dreamed one winter night, a new piano she touched had turned, after the one pristine moment, into a calling cow, it was by her own desire (*CS*, p. 453).

The night after her mother's funeral, Virgie is roused from bed by a pounding on the porch-floor outside. Trembling, she goes to the door in her nightgown and finds an old country woman with a night-blooming cereus to give her. The strange old crone has appeared out of the night to present an erotic feminine flower as a tribute to Virgie's former beauty and her music. The flower acts as an image to connect Virgie's music to the yearnings she senses in the cows. 'Virgie looked at the naked, luminous, complicated flower, large and pale as a face on the dark porch. For a moment she felt more afraid than she had coming to the door' (CS, p. 453).

Virgie's fear persists after the old woman has disappeared into the darkness but, as she throws the troubling flower down into the weeds, she has a comforting vision of her daughterly connection with the river and the maternal moon.

> She knew that now at the river, where she had been before on moonlit nights in autumn, drunken and sleepless, mist lay on the water and filled the trees, and from the eyes to the moon would be a cone, a long silent horn, of white light. It was a connection visible as the hair is in air, between the self and the moon, to make the self feel the child, a daughter far, far back (CS, p. 454).

This vision, made possible by the gift of the night flower, helps us to fully understand Virgie's evening swim the day before as a reintegration into ancient maternal forces represented by the moon, forces which can assuage the yearnings and pain of a woman's life which can find no appropriate relief in ordinary experience.

The final scene of *The Golden Apples* attempts a reconciliation of opposites, but it is not conclusive. Virgie Rainey has paused in the nearby town of MacLain on her way out of Morgana to begin a new life. A gentle rain falls on the MacLain cemetery and the surrounding world, very similar to the snow falling everywhere at the end of Joyce's 'The Dead', as Albert Devlin has remarked.[8] Welty's rain suggests modesty and tolerance in Virgie's mind similar to the feelings of Joyce's Gabriel Conroy as he watches from his Dublin hotel room at the gentle snow falling all over Ireland and softening harsh objects on the landscape. Virgie gains a perspective which will allow her to live the rest of her life in a kind of harmony with the opposing forces represented by the intolerable demands of Miss Eckhart on the one hand and Virgie's own natural instincts on the other. Virgie has always been driven by natural energies similar to those motivating King MacLain, and thus she has thought she hated Miss Eckhart for trying to force her into the rigid discipline of a musical career. Now in the rain Virgie understands the significance of Miss Eckhart's emblematic picture of Perseus and Medusa.

> Miss Eckhart, whom Virgie had not, after all, hated – had come near to loving, for she had taken Miss Eckhart's hate, and then her love, extracted them, the thorn and then the overflow – had hung the picture on the wall for herself. [Miss Eckhart] had absorbed the hero and the victim and then, stoutly, could sit down to the piano with all Beethoven ahead of her. With her hate, with her love, and with the small gnawing feelings that ate them, she offered Virgie her Beethoven. She offered, offered, offered – and when Virgie was young, in the strange wisdom of youth that is accepting of more than is given, she had accepted *the* Beethoven, as with the dragon's blood. That was the gift she had touched with her fingers that had drifted and left her (*CS*, p. 460).

Virgie finally understands Miss Eckhart as an androgynous combination of both the male hero and the powerful female sacrificed to him. In myth, Pegasus sprang from the blood of the murdered Gorgon, so that Medusa's power assumed a new embodiment in the magic steed who became the horse of the Muses. Miss Eckhart's absorption of *both* hero and victim in the myth therefore implies that she inherits its

offspring, Pegasus, who represents the agency of artistic
power for her performance of Beethoven's music.

By confronting Miss Eckhart's influence, Virgie has
confronted and understood the critical choice she made
in her own life. At the end of *The Golden Apples* she is a
self-styled exile, freed by her mother's death and sharing
her temporary shelter from the rain with an old black beggar
woman in this final scene. These two feminine wanderers
hear a message which affirms their relation to wild and
fabled creatures of mystery and power. 'They heard through
falling rain the running of the horse and bear, the stroke of
the leopard, the dragon's crusty slither, and the glimmer
and the trumpet of the swan' (*CS*, p. 461).

The Golden Apples offers no firm evidence about what
Virgie's life will become after her mother's death, but it
will probably continue to be uncommitted and searching.
In *The Optimist's Daughter*, Welty examines the fate of
a woman from another small Mississippi town who has
committed herself to her art and thus does not suffer
Virgie's restlessness. Laurel Hand is about Virgie's age,
and while she differs in social class and in character, she
seems to extend Welty's exploration of some of the issues
left unresolved in the earlier book. 'One may have led to
the other,' Welty has said. 'Virgie and Laurel were such
different people, backgrounds and everything, but they
were doing the same thing' in coming to terms with their
memories at the end of their stories.[9]

The Optimist's Daughter echoes many familiar themes
from *Delta Wedding* and *The Golden Apples*, especially
in its emphasis on family gatherings for important rituals
such as weddings and funerals, in the motif of the brash
and determined lower-class women who capture beloved
males of prominent families, and in the emphasis on
the abandoning of old traditions in favour of new trends
represented by suburban housing tracts and interstate
highways. Most important for our purposes among all

these familiar materials is the troubled relationship between mother and daughter whose resolution is essential for the main character's knowledge of herself, as it was in *The Golden Apples*. Virgie Rainey could not finally face the past and silence its claims until her ties to her mother had been dissolved, and similarly Laurel Hand is forced by her father's death and the antics of his abrasive new wife, Fay Chisom, to reevaluate the bitter despair of her dying mother Becky. In understanding and grieving for her mother and grandmother, and in seeing the similarities between her relation to her mother and her mother's daughterly role with her grandmother, Laurel is enabled to face the grief of her own buried past. When she accepts the loss of her parents and her husband Phil, Laurel frees herself to return to her independent life as a fashion designer in Chicago, leaving the old family house and possessions behind with Fay in Mount Salus, Mississippi.

In some ways *The Optimist's Daughter* seems to have served for Eudora Welty a purpose similar to the one John Griffin Jones described for Laurel's final recovery and release of the breadboard her husband had carefully crafted for her mother, an object that represents her 'whole solid past'. Welty agreed with Jones's comment that when Laurel leaves the breadboard with Fay, 'she is making a commitment through memory to her future, she is able to live on without being drowned by memory.[10] Just as Virgie Rainey put her mother's spirit to rest on the evening of her swim and Miss Eckhart's memory to rest in the MacLain graveyard in the rain, Laurel Hand makes a peace with her mother's ghost in *The Optimist's Daughter*.

What precipitates Laurel's encounter with her mother's accusing spirit is the shock of her stepmother's vulgar scene at her father's funeral. Ironically, Fay makes a spectacular protest against death that reveals her daughterly relation to her own mother, fat old Mrs Chisom, who has arrived unexpectedly from Texas in a pickup truck with a large representation of the unruly Chisom clan for the funeral. Fay had earlier lied about her family, claiming that they were all dead and that she would never have abandoned ageing parents as Laurel did, for what Fay calls selfish reasons of ambition. Yet that is exactly what Fay had done in leaving Texas to make her fortune as a typist in Mississippi. She defied her mother in order to make a new life for herself, but, *in extremis* at the funeral of her elderly husband, she acts as her mother would. She stalks into the parlour full of mourners where Judge McKelva lies on display in a pink, satin-lined coffin. Glistening in black satin and high heels herself, Fay reacts to the surprise appearance of her mother and sister by crying, 'Get back! – Who told *them* to come?' Fay turns her back on her mother and cries to the dead judge, 'O, hon, get up, get out of there. . . . '

'Can't you hear me, hon?' called Fay.

'She's cracking,' said Mrs Chisom. 'Just like me. Poor little Wanda Fay.'

'Oh, Judge, how could you be so unfair to me?' Fay cried. . . . 'Oh, Judge, how could you go off and leave me this way? Why did you want to treat me so unfair?'

Genteel old family friends try to calm Fay, but she breaks wildly away and throws herself at the coffin. One of the judge's contemporaries, an imposing old matriarch, drags Fay screaming out of the room, while Mrs Chisom's voice drives through the confusion: 'Like mother, like daughter. Though when I had to give up her dad, they couldn't hold me half so easy. I tore up the whole house, I did' (*OD*, pp. 84–6). The vital bond between Fay and her poor-white family is affirmed by this behaviour, and Fay returns with her family for a brief visit to Texas after the funeral.

Laurel is left alone in her parents' house with her memories for the last time. That night she confronts the unresolved anguish of her past in the tiny sewing-room where she has sought refuge from a chimney-swift trapped in the house. The bird represents the dangerous forces of memory unleashed in Laurel's mind by the funeral day's events. Laurel finds many mementos of her parents' lives in the little room, and the past floods back. Chiefly she remembers her mother's life in the West Virginia mountains 'up home' where Becky had taken her many childhood summers to visit her grandmother. Welty has said that all this West Virginia material is autobiographical, and it seems probable that writing the novel allowed Welty to recover and evaluate some of her own past through Laurel Hand. Laurel's mother Becky is based on Welty's mother, sharing the same West Virginia background, the early experience as a mountain schoolteacher, interest in gardening and playing bridge with old friends and the same debilitating eye problems and subsequent operations. But Welty insists on our recognising that these similarities do not make Becky McKelva a fictional portrait of Chestina Welty; 'the character of Becky, the mother, is not the character of my mother, but it draws upon it'.[11]

Laurel thinks back to cosy scenes with her mother in the sewing room which must be close to Eudora Welty's own experience. 'Firelight and warmth – that was what her memory gave her.' She pictures her mother sitting at the old treadle sewing-machine, while she sat as a little girl and made stories out of scraps of cloth. This process is a clear feminine metaphor for Welty's own career as a maker of stories.

When her mother. . . sat here in her chair pedalling and whirring, Laurel sat on this floor and put together the fallen scraps of cloth into stars, flowers, birds, people, or whatever she liked to call them, lining them up, spacing them out, making them into patterns, families, on the sweet-smelling matting, with the shine of firelight, or the summer light, moving over mother and child and what they both were making (*OD*, pp. 133–4).

From this idyllic picture of mother and daughter, Laurel moves back to images of summer 'up home' in one of those wide, sweeping vistas Ellen Moers finds to be particularly feminine landscapes.

Bird dogs went streaking through the upslanting pasture through the sweet long grass that swept them as high as their noses. While it was still day on top of the mountain, the light still warm on the cheek, the valley was dyed blue under them. While one of 'the boys' was coming up, his white shirt would shine for a long time almost without moving in her sight, like Venus in the sky of Mount Salus, while grandmother, mother, and little girl sat, out-lasting the light, waiting for him to climb home (*OD*, p. 139).

Welty explained to Jan Nordby Gretlund that this was a scene from her own early childhood. 'The way my uncles looked coming home at night through the far-off fields, just white shirts showing down the mountain. . . . I still recall this, and I just put it all in there.'[12]

Laurel's memory fixes on her grandmother's pigeons, who taught her a terrible truth about human dependency. As a small girl she had seen the birds, 'sticking their beaks down each other's throats, gagging each other, eating out of each other's craws, swallowing down all over again what had been swallowed before: they were taking turns'. Even as a child, Laurel understood the relevance of this scene for human relationships. 'Parents and children take turns back and forth, changing places, protecting and protesting each other; so it seemed to the child' (*OD*, p. 141). Adulthood has given her detailed experience of the process, and as a grieving middle-aged woman, she now confronts the pain

of loss when this reciprocal dependency is dissolved by
death. Laurel's own mother had cried uncontrollably when
she learned of her mother's death up in the West Virginia
mountains. When Becky herself came to die, she began
bitterly accusing her husband of not being able to sustain
her. The pigeons might have taken turns protecting and
protesting each other, but against the onslaught of death
their human analogues were helpless. 'Why do you persist
in letting them hurt me?' Laurel's mother would demand
during her five years of increasing blindness and pain.
Suddenly Laurel realises that her own husband Phil, killed
as a young man in the war, might have similarly protested.
This understanding develops out of her bonds with other
women, her ability to evaluate the relations between her
grandmother, her mother and herself. She finds crumbling
old letters from her grandmother to her mother and sees a
similarity between her mother's rebellion and independence
from the grandmother's world and her own choice of an
independent life in Chicago, far from the family home
in Mississippi: 'Widowed, her health failing, lonely and
sometimes bedridden, Grandma wrote these letters to her
young, venturesome, defiant, happily married daughter as
to an exile, without ever allowing herself to put it into so
many words' (*OD*, p. 153).

The final message in the letters is the key to the
climactic revelation of this night of grief, and the letter
echoes the language of two letters that Welty quotes
from her own grandmother in *One Writer's Beginnings*.[13]
'I will try to send Laurel a cup of sugar for her birthday.
Though if I can find a way to do it, I would like to send
her one of my pigeons. It would eat from her hand, if she
would let it' (*OD*, p. 154). The grandmother understands
her grand-daughter's fastidiousness about human commit-
ments but wishes to help her accept their grotesque
give-and-take by association with the pigeons. Laurel
understands the point in a flash, which brings back with

terrible urgency the desperate need of her husband for his unlived life.

A flood of feeling descended on Laurel. She let the papers slide from her hand and the books from her knees, and put her head down on the open lid of the desk and wept for love and for the dead. She lay there with all that was adamant in her yielding to this night, yielding at last. Now all she had found had found her. The deepest spring in her heart had uncovered itself, and it began to flow again.

If Phil could have lived —

But Phil was lost. Nothing of their life together remained except in her own memory; love was sealed away into its perfection and had remained there.

If Phil had lived — (*OD*, p. 154).

After all the years of independent widowhood, the perfection of this memory is shattered. 'Now, by her own hands, the past had risen up, and *he* looked at her, Phil himself – here waiting, all the time, Lazarus. He looked at her out of eyes wild with the craving for his unlived life, with mouth open like a funnel's.' Through her mother's grief, Laurel has reached her own, and now she faces again the raw anguish of her most intimate grief and must accept the fact that it can never be assuaged.

The next morning, however, she has absorbed this truth, and she prepares to return to her life in Chicago. Through the agency of the breadboard, she finally frees herself from her past, leaving it behind with Fay, who has absolutely no comprehension of its meaning. The finely crafted board is a repository of memory because Phil had made it as a special gift for Laurel's mother and Becky had used it for kneading her excellent bread. Two kinds of loving craft, masculine carpentry and feminine baking, are united in the object which has stood years of affectionate family service. Insensitive Fay, who seems to have no domestic skills, has defaced the board by cracking nuts on it with a hammer. When Fay disputes Laurel's right to take the breadboard away with her from Mount Salus, the clash of their attitudes toward the past reveals a crucial difference in their abilities to live in the present.

Both women have moved away from their mothers, venturing out to professional lives far from the family home and abandoning traditional domestic models of womanhood, but Laurel never denied her mother's values or the nourishing traditions of the past. Fay, in contrast, never admitted the existence of her family until the crowd of Chisoms unexpectedly arrived in their pickup truck for Judge McKelva's funeral. Her reaction to seeing her mother and sister is less than friendly, and her trip back to Texas with them seems more a method of ensuring their departure than an expression of affection. Once she is back in Mount Salus again after her three-day visit with her family, she seems to have completely forgotten them. 'The past isn't a thing to me,' she declared to Laurel. 'I belong to the future, didn't you know that?' (*OD*, p. 179).

Welty explained to an interviewer that such an attitude afflicts its bearers. 'If they had memory it would've taught them something about the present. They have nothing to draw on. They don't understand their own experience.'[14] At the end of *The Optimist's Daughter*, Laurel sees that Fay 'was without any powers of passion or imagination in herself and had no way to see it or reach it in the other person. Other people, inside their lives, might as well be invisible to her' (*OD*, p. 178).

Laurel's time in Mount Salus has brought her memories back with a painful acuity which helps her to understand not only her dead parents and husband, but even her grasping, vindictive stepmother. She realises, as Fay denies the past, that memory 'will come back in its wounds from across the world, like Phil, calling us by our names and demanding its rightful tears'. Surrendering to grief brings understanding and peace. Thus Laurel can forgive Fay, leave the bread-board behind on the kitchen table and relinquish her claim to the objects which belonged to her past. Her confrontation with Fay has taught her that memory 'lived not in initial possession but in the freed hands, pardoned and freed, and in the heart that can empty but fill again, in the patterns restored by dreams' (*OD*, pp. 178–80). Laurel's old friends urge her to give up her job in Chicago and return to live out her life with them in the old familiar setting, taking her mother's place in their bridge game as in their lives. But Laurel knows that she does not belong in Mount Salus. She has long ago established a solid independent life for herself in the North by building on the values her parents transmitted to her in childhood. These are symbolised by the one object she takes away with her – a little stone boat carved 'up home' by her father when he was courting her mother. Unlike the breadboard, which is a feminine tool of another time and representative of other roles, the little boat, carved by her father from the very stone of Becky's mountain landscape, is a symbol of movement which the daughter takes away to another life built on the living foundation of memory.

6 Welty's Affirmations

Eudora Welty's long career has brought her respect, affection and, in recent years, more public regard than most writers achieve. But she has not yet been accorded the serious attention of the academic community outside the American South, because the comic, affirmative mode in which she writes and the grounding of her work in women's experience has led many critics to dismiss it as sentimental, merely charming or trivial. Elizabeth Bowen's 1947 praise for the 'heart-breaking sweetness' in *Delta Wedding* and its 'sense of the momentum, joy, pain and mystery of life' defines qualities of affirmation which mark most of Welty's fiction but which are unfashionable in the 'Postmodern Age'. Women writers have commonly been charged with sentimentality and triviality for concentrating on domestic relationships and female experience, but the feminist revolution in literary criticism is gradually shifting the criteria for determining literary value. The same kind of attention that moved Virginia Woolf to the forefront of twentieth-century English fiction is beginning to be applied to Eudora Welty. Almost ten years ago, critics like Peggy Prenshaw and Margaret Bolsterli first called attention to Welty's particular focus on women's experience. Patricia Yaeger has more recently examined Welty's radical questioning of patriarchal power in *The Golden Apples*, and in another work I have explored Welty's celebration of traditional female power and its mythic basis in *Delta Wedding*.[1] Welty's skill as a prose stylist is thus increasingly understood to

serve a major new feminine vision in American literature
which challenges the traditional masculine emphasis upon
solitary, agonistic heroism and the escape from civilisation
and the feminine.

As Cassie Morrison realises in 'June Recital', 'Some performances of people stayed partly untold for lack of a name,
. . . as well as for lack of believers' (*CS*, p. 296). Through
a comedy of manners that conceals its own complex and
versatile art, Eudora Welty has told of many hilarious
and terrible performances in women's lives and the lives
of the men who live with many of them. She has given
voice to the consciousness of people like the old black
grandmother of 'A Worn Path', the entrapped and yearn-
ing spinsters Clytie and Jenny Lockhart, the despairing
males of 'Flowers for Marjorie' and 'Death of a Traveling
Salesman' who cannot share the fullness of women's
experience in childbearing, the mothers and daughters of
Delta Wedding and *The Optimist's Daughter*, the ladies in
small-town beauty parlours and eccentric postmistresses.
If successful marriages have been dramatised, so also have
failures of love and eruptions of sexual violence in rape and
murder. Overall, however, Welty's fiction testifies to the
resilience of the human community nourished by feminine
strength.

Welty reaches back through myth to recover long
traditions of female self-sufficiency and strength that
have been deliberately obscured by patriarchal culture. She
demonstrates that despite the cultural propaganda of the
past three or four thousand years, the world of women has
preserved its older heritage of sustenance and cooperation
– that in fact, civilisation continues *because* of these values.
Demeter and Kore is a much older myth than Oedipus, and
in *Delta Wedding*, Welty restores it to its central place in our
culture.

And she does not stop there. She retrieves treasures
from our past so that we can integrate them with our

present situations, but as her later portraits of daughters show – in *The Golden Apples* and *The Optimist's Daughter* – women must now voyage out to create new forms. Welty cannot dramatise what modes of action they will create or what they will find. Virgie Rainey is left poised on the fence, and Laurel Hand's life in Chicago is never described. But both these daughters of the modern world are on the move. Younger writers are already telling us where they are going. These women are breaking traditional gender definitions apart, reshaping them, and writing about the ways contemporary women are defining their lives. They owe much to Welty's explorations of the possibilities before them.

Eudora Welty's profound commitment to her art has led her in explorations whose full significance she probably does not recognise herself. Uneasy with political crusading of any kind, she has sought to explore the landscapes of the heart as fully as her instincts and observations could enable her to do. We have seen how completely they are centred on women's experience, but that orientation appears to be one that she did not consciously seek. In typically modest terms, she describes a little night-light, like the one Dabney Fairchild receives and then heedlessly breaks in *Delta Wedding*, as the metaphor for fiction itself.

> Some of us grew up with the china night-light, the little lamp whose lighting showed its secret and with that spread enchantment. The outside is painted with a scene, which is one thing; then, when the lamp is lighted, through the porcelain sides a new picture comes out through the old, and they are seen as one. . . . The lamp alight is the combination of internal and external, glowing at the imagination as one; and so is the good novel. Seeing that these inner and outer surfaces do lie so close together and so implicit in each other, the wonder is that human life so often separates them, or apppears to,

and it takes a good novel to put them back together (*Eye*,
p. 120).

Her stories and novels bring the inner and outer life back
into communication with each other, providing readers with
the inner illumination of experience that is at once centrally
feminine and broadly human.

Notes

Notes to Chapter 1

1. *Conversations with Eudora Welty*, ed. Peggy Whitman Prenshaw (Jackson, University Press of Mississippi, 1984), p. 54. All subsequent citations to this book will be indicated by the abbreviation *CNVRS* and page number in my text.

2. *The Eye of the Story: Selected Essays and Reviews* (New York, Random House, 1978), pp. 146–58.

3. *One Writer's Beginnings* (Cambridge and London, Harvard University Press, 1984), p. 104. All subsequent citations of this book will appear in my text with the abbreviation *OWB* and page number.

4. Conversation with Eudora Welty in her home, 16 June 1987; see also *OWB*, p. 51.

5. *Eudora*, photographic exhibit selected and edited by Patti Carr Black (Jackson, Mississippi Department of Archives and History, 1984), p. 16; *OWB*, pp. 4–5.

6. *OWB*, pp. 8–9; BBC *Omnibus* video, *A Writer's Beginnings*, Mississippi Department of Archives and History.

7. *OWB*, pp. 100–101; Ruth M. Vande Kieft, *Eudora Welty* (Boston, Twayne, 1987), p. 4; the experience of framing her vision with her hands, described in the quotation from 'A Memory' in *OWB*, pp. 87–9, is surely autobiographical, although what the narrator saw in the story was fiction.

8. *Literary Women* (New York, Doubleday, 1976), pp. 259–63.

9. W. J. Cash, *The Mind of the South* (New York, Alfred Knopf, 1941), pp. 86–7.

10. *CNVRS*, pp. 176–7; *OWB*, pp. 76–81; Vande Kieft, op. cit., pp. 4–5.

11. Alfred Kazin, *On Native Grounds* (New York, Reynal and Hitchcock, 1947), pp. 501–502.

12. Elizabeth Evans, *Eudora Welty* (New York, Ungar, 1981), pp. 7–9.

13. Welty Correspondence, Box #1, Folders 1–4, Mississippi Department of Archives and History; *CNVRS*, pp. 146–7.

14. 1 November, 1937, Welty Correspondence, Box #1, Folders 1–4, Mississippi Department of Archives and History; *CNVRS*, pp. 146–7.

15. R. N. Linscott, 28 May 1938, Welty Correspondence, Box #1, Folder 3.

16. Welty Correspondence, Box #1; *CNVRS*, p. 81.

17. Welty Correspondence, Box #1, Folders 3–4.

18. Welty Correspondence, Box #1, Folder 4; *CNVRS*, 40–42.

19. Vande Kieft, 'Chronology', in *Eudora Welty*, op. cit., unpaginated; Virginia Spencer Carr, *The Lonely Hunter: A Biography of Carson McCullers* (New York, Doubleday, 1975), figures 66, 71, 72; Welty Correspondence, Box #2, Folder 1.

20. Conversation with Eudora Welty, Jackson, Mississippi, 18 June 1987.

21. 'Delta Wedding', Reviews, Eudora Welty Collection, Mississippi Department of Archives and History; *The Tatler*, 6 August 1947, p. 183.

22. Welty Correspondence, Box #2, Folder 3; Conversations with Eudora Welty in Jackson, 18 June and 16 September 1987.

23. 'A Conversation with Eudora Welty, Jackson, 1986', interviewers Albert J. Devlin and Peggy Whitman Prenshaw, *Mississippi Quarterly* [Special Welty Issue] (Fall 1986), pp. 430–35.

24. Elizabeth Evans, op. cit., p. xii.

25. 'A Conversation with Eudora Welty, Jackson, 1986', interviewers Albert J. Devlin and Peggy Whitman Prenshaw, op. cit., p. 440.

26. Welty Correspondence, Box #2, Folder 4; and Box #3 (uncalendared letters to John Robinson which can be dated fall, 1948 and spring, 1949 by internal evidence); Evans, op. cit., p. 16

27. Welty Correspondence, Box #3.

Notes to Chapter 2

1. 'The Radiance of Jane Austen' in *The Eye of the Story* (New York, Random House, 1978), p. 6.

2. *Images of the South: Visits with Eudora Welty and Walker Evans*, Intro. by Bill Ferris, Southern Folklore Reports 1 (Memphis: Center for Southern Folklore, 1977), p. 13.

3. Ellen Moers, *Literary Women* (New York, Doubleday, 1976), pp. 42–62.

4. Jane Marcus, paper presented at the Modern Language Association of America, 1982.

5. Virginia Woolf, *A Room of One's Own* (Harmondsworth, Penguin, 1965), p. 87.

6. Harold Bloom, *The Anxiety of Influence* (New York, Oxford University Press, 1973); for a feminist perspective on the problem of influence, see Sandra Gilbert and Susan Gubar, *The Madwoman in the Attic: The Woman Writer and the Nineteenth-Century Literary Imagination* (New Haven, Yale University Press, 1979), pp. 1–70.

7. Bowen, *The Tatler and Bystander* (6 August 1947), p. 183.

8. See Sterling North, *New York Post* (18 April 1946); Isaac Rosenfeld,

The New Republic (29 April 1946); and an anonymous reviewer in *The Providence Journal* (14 April 1946).

9. Philip Fisher, *Hard Facts* (New York, Oxford, 1985), pp. 22–86.

10. *The American Adam* (Chicago, University of Chicago Press, 1955); *The Machine in the Garden: Technology and the Pastoral Ideal in America* (New York, Oxford, 1978); and *The Lay of the Land: Metaphor as Experience and History in American Life and Letters* (Chapel Hill, University of North Carolina Press, 1975).

11. Nancy Armstrong, *Desire and Domestic Fiction* (New York, Oxford, 1987).

12. Leslie Fiedler, *The Inadvertent Epic* (New York, Simon and Schuster, 1979); Ann Douglas, *The Feminization of American Culture* (New York, Alfred Knopf, 1977); and Jane Tompkins, *Sensational Designs: The Cultural Work of American Fiction* (New York, Oxford University Press, 1985).

13. 'Is the Gaze Male?' in Ann Snitow *et al.* (eds), *Powers of Desire: The Politics of Sexuality* (New York, Monthly Review Press, 1983), pp. 309–25.

14. *The Collected Stories of Eudora Welty* (New York, Harcourt Brace Jovanovich, 1980), pp. 373–4. All further citations will be made with the abbreviation *CS* and page number in my text.

15. 'The Daughter's Seduction: Sexual Violence and Literary History', *Signs* (Summer, 1986), 629–33.

16. Patricia Yaeger, ' "Because a Fire Was in My Head": Eudora Welty and the Dialogic Imagination', *Publications of the Modern Language Association* (October 1984), pp. 955–73.

17. Conversation with Eudora Welty, Jackson, Mississippi, 16 September 1987.

18. Conversation with Eudora Welty, Jackson, Mississippi, 16 June 1987; Letter from Dale Mullen, 7 June 1937, Welty Correspondence, Box #1, Folder 2.

19. Edward Kessler, *Flannery O'Connor and the Language of Apocalypse* (Princeton, Princeton University Press, 1986), pp. 24–9.

20. Conversation with Eudora Welty, Jackson, Mississippi, 16 June 1987.

21. Diana Trilling, 'Fiction in Review', *The Nation* (22 September 1943); Bowen, op. cit.

22. Conversations with Eudora Welty, Jackson, Mississippi, 16 June and 16 September 1987; see also 'A Conversation with Eudora Welty, Jackson, 1986', ed. Albert J. Devlin and Peggy Whitman Prenshaw, op. cit., pp. 436–7.

23. 'A Conversation with Eudora Welty', Devlin and Prenshaw, op. cit., p. 447.

24. *The Optimist's Daughter* (New York, Random House, 1972), pp. 159–60. All subsequent references to this book will be in my text with the abbreviation *OD* and page number.

Notes to Chapter 3

1. Erskine Caldwell and Margaret Bourke-White, *You Have Seen Their Faces* (New York, Viking Press, 1937); Dorothea Lange and Paul Taylor, *An American Exodus* (New York, Reynal and Hitchcock, 1939); Richard Wright and Edwin Rosskam, *12 Million Black Voices* (New York, Viking Press, 1941); and James Agee and Walter Evans, *Let Us Now Praise Famous Men* (Boston, Houghton, Mifflin, 1941).

2. Julia Peterkin and Doris Ulmann, *Roll Jordan, Roll* (New York, R. O. Ballou, 1933).

3. *One Time, One Place* (New York, Random House, 1971), p. 6. All subsequent references to this book will be made in my text with the abbreviation *OTOP* and page number.

4. Wright and Rosskam, op. cit., p. 35.

5. 'Literature and the Lens', *Vogue*, 104 (1 August 1944), pp. 102–103.

6. *A Writer's Beginnings*, op. cit.

7. Robert Penn Warren 'The Love and Separateness in Miss Welty', *Kenyon Review* (Spring 1944), pp. 246–59.

8. Ruth Vande Kieft, *Eudora Welty*, op. cit., p. 46. See this book for the first authoritative interpretations of Welty's short fiction to appear. The study was originally published in 1962.

9. Robert Penn Warren, 'The Love and Separateness in Miss Welty', op. cit pp. 246–7.

Notes to Chapter 4

1. Michael Kreyling, *Eudora Welty's Achievement of Order* (Baton Rouge, Louisiana State University Press, 1980), p. 55

2. Conversations with Eudora Welty, Jackson, Mississippi, 16 June and 16 September 1987.

3. '*Delta Wedding* as Region and Symbol', *Sewanee Review* (Summer, 1952), pp. 397–417.

4. See R. W. B. Lewis, *The American Adam* (Chicago, University of Chicago Press, 1955); Leslie Fiedler, *Love and Death in the American Novel* (New York, Criterion, 1960); and Leo Marx, *The Machine in the Garden* (New York, Oxford, 1978).

5. See Philip Fisher, *Hard Facts* (New York, Oxford, 1985), pp. 3–86.

6. Vande Kieft (op. cit., p. 83) and Kreyling (op. cit., p. 61) have commented on the symbolic meaning of the name 'Shellmound'. Historical information can be found in the Mississippi Department of Archives and History in Jackson, where Annie H. Dixon presents a detailed history of the mound Welty placed in *Delta Wedding*, in File 610: 'Shellmound, Leflore County'. The geographical distribution of the mounds is discussed in the subject file 'Indian Mounds', which also includes an essay, 'Indian Mounds of Mississippi', explaining Choctaw legends concerning them.

7. Conversation with Eudora Welty, Jackson, Mississippi, 16 June 1987.

8. *To the Lighthouse* (New York, Harcourt Brace, 1927), p. 45.

9. G. S. Kirk, *The Nature of Greek Myths* (New York, Penguin Books, 1980), pp. 248–53; Jaan Puhvel, 'Eleuther and Oinoatis: Dyonysiac Data from Mycenaean Greece', in Emmett L. Bennett, Jr (ed.), *Mycenaean Studies* (Madison, University of Wisconsin Press, 1964), pp. 161–9; *The Bacchae of Euripides*, trans. G. S. Kirk (New York, Cambridge University Press, 1979), pp. 28, 81–3.

10. Hesiod, *The Homeric Hymns and Homerica*, trans. H. G. Evelyn-White (Cambridge, Harvard University Press, 1974), p. 457.

11. Moers, *Literary Women*, op. cit., pp. 257–62.

12. C. Kerenyi, *Eleusis: Archetypal Images of Mother and Daughter*, trans. by Ralph Manheim (New York, Schocken Books, 1977), pp. 34–5, 356–69; and George E. Mylonas, *The Hymn to Demeter and Her Sanctuary at Eleusis* (St Louis, Washington University Studies, 1942), p. 3.

13. John Alexander Allen, 'The Other Way to Live: Demigods in Eudora Welty's Fiction', in *Eudora Welty: Critical Essays*, ed. Peggy Whitman Prenshaw (Jackson, University Press of Mississippi, 1979), p. 29.

14. Kreyling, op. cit., pp. 72–6.

15. Conversation with Eudora Welty, Jackson, Mississippi, 16 June 1987.

16. Prenshaw, 'Woman's World, Man's Place', in *Eudora Welty: A Form of Thanks*, ed. Louis Dollarhide (Jackson, University Press of Mississippi, 1979), p. 50; Welty, *Eye*, op. cit., p. 120.

Notes to Chapter 5

1. Discussed by Rebecca Mark in 'From Rape Victim to Artist: Eudora Welty's Creation of Female Voice in *The Golden Apples*', Modern Language Association of America, 28 December 1987, San Francisco, California.

2. Vande Kieft, op. cit., p. 91.

3. Patricia Yaeger sees this episode in somewhat different terms, finding that while Welty parodies Yeats's poem and quarrels 'with Yeats's mythology of gender', she nevertheless reminds us that 'women's desire is still inscribed by a male economy'; op. cit., pp. 960–61.

4. For fuller treatment of Welty's use of Yeats's poem, see Vande Kieft, op. cit., pp. 87–125; Kreyling, op. cit., pp. 77–105; Evans, op. cit., pp. 63–76; and Yaeger, op. cit., pp. 965–8.

5. 'The Case of the Dangling Signifier: Phallic Imagery in "Moon Lake"', *Twentieth Century Literature* (Winter, 1982), pp. 431–52. See also Kreyling, op. cit., p. 90.

6. Yaeger, op. cit., p. 441.

7. See Chapter 2, pp. 40–41.

8. Albert Devlin, *Eudora Welty's Chronicle: A Story of Mississippi Life* (Jackson, The University Press of Mississippi, 1983), p. 204.

9. *CNVRS*, op. cit., p. 335.

10. *CNVRS*, op. cit., p. 335.

11. *CNVRS*, op. cit., p. 116; see also pp. 69 and 175.

12. *CNVRS*, op. cit., p. 213.

13. *OWB*, pp. 54–7.

14. *CNVRS*, op. cit., p. 336.

Note to Chapter 6

1. See Louis Dollarhide and Ann J. Abadie (eds), *Eudora Welty: A Form of Thanks* (Jackson, University Press of Mississippi, 1979); Peggy W. Prenshaw (ed.), *Eudora Welty: Critical Essays* (Jackson, University Press of Mississippi); Yaeger, op. cit.; and Westling, *Sacred Groves and Ravaged Gardens: The Fiction of Eudora Welty, Carson McCullers and Flannery O'Connor* (Athens, Georgia, University of Georgia Press, 1985).

Bibliography

Selected Works by Eudora Welty

The Bride of Innisfallen (New York, Harcourt Brace, 1955).
The Collected Stories of Eudora Welty (New York and London, Harcourt Brace Jovanovich, 1980).
A Curtain of Green and Other Stories (New York, Doubleday, 1941).
Delta Wedding (New York, Harcourt Brace, 1946).
The Eye of the Story: Selected Essays and Reviews (New York, Random House, 1971).
The Golden Apples (New York, Harcourt Brace, 1949).
Losing Battles (New York, Random House, 1970).
One Time, One Place: Mississippi in the Depression (New York, Random House, 1971).
One Writer's Beginnings (Cambridge, Massachusetts, Harvard University Press, 1984).
The Optimist's Daughter (New York, Random House, 1972).
The Ponder Heart (New York, Random House, 1954).
The Robber Bridegroom (New York, Doubleday, 1943).
The Wide Net and Other Stories (New York, Harcourt Brace, 1943).

Selected Works About Eudora Welty

Books listed here are those which the author has found most useful in defining and interpreting Eudora Welty's work. Some more specialised criticism and related scholarship, as for instance that having to do with mythology, is cited in the Notes but not listed here. Most books in this list contain useful bibliographies indicating archival materials, checklists, reviews, and articles about particular works or critical approaches.

Desmond, John, *A Still Moment: Essays on the Art of Eudora Welty* (Metuchen, New Jersey, Scarecrow Press, 1978).
Devlin Albert J., *Eudora Welty's Chronicle: A Story of Mississippi Life* (Jackson, University Press of Mississippi, 1983).
Devlin, Albert J. (ed.), *Welty: A Life in Literature* (Jackson and London, University Press of Mississippi, 1987).

Dollarhide, Louis, and Ann J. Abadie (eds), *Eudora Welty: A Form of Thanks* (Jackson, University Press of Mississippi, 1979).

Evans, Elizabeth, *Eudora Welty* (New York, Frederick Ungar, 1981).

Kreyling, Michael, *Eudora Welty's Achievement of Order* (Baton Rouge, Louisiana State University Press, 1980).

Manning, Carol Sue, *With Ears Opening Like Morning Glories: Eudora Welty and the Love of Story Telling* (Westport, Connecticut, Greenwood Press, 1985).

Prenshaw, Peggy Whitman (ed.), *Conversations with Eudora Welty* (Jackson, University Press of Mississippi, 1984).

Prenshaw, Peggy Whitman (ed.), *Eudora Welty: Critical Essays* (Jackson, University Press of Mississippi, 1979).

Swearingen, Bethany, *Eudora Welty, A Critical Bibliography, 1936–1958* (Jackson, University Press of Mississippi, 1984).

Thompson, Victor H. *Eudora Welty: A Reference Guide* (Boston, G. K. Hall, 1976).

Vande Kieft, Ruth M., *Eudora Welty* (Boston, Twayne, 1987).

Index